# SHIRE

Angela Thompson Smith

Copyright © 2019 by Angela Thompson Smith

All rights reserved. No part of this publication may be reproduced, distributed, or transmitted in any form or by any means, including photocopying, recording or other electronic or mechanical methods, without the prior written permission of the publisher, except in the case of brief quotations embodied in critical reviews and certain other noncommercial uses permitted under copyright law. For permission requests contact the publisher, addressed. Attention: "Permissions Coordinator" at the address below.

Editor: Mindwise Press
(702) 417-6154
mindwiseconsulting@gmail.com

First Printing, 2006
Second Printing: 2019

ISBN: 9781093283372

Also published by Angela Thompson Smith:

*'Remote Perceptions: Out of Body Experiences, Remote Viewing, and Other Normal Abilities,'* 2nd Ed., 2017, Triangulum Publishing. (1st edition; 1998 by Hampton Roads Publishing).

*'Diary of an Abduction: A Scientist Probes the Enigma of her Alien Contact,'* 2001, Hampton Roads Publishing. (Out of Print).

*'River of Passion,'* 2007, Publish America. (Out of Print).

*'Voices from the Cosmos,'* with co-author C. B. Scott Jones Ph.D. 2014, Headline Books.

*'Seer: 30 Years of Remote Viewing; and Counting,'* 2017, Triangulum Publishing.

*'Colombia Quest,'* 2018, Triangulum Publishing.

*'Tactical Remote Viewing'* 2019, Mindwise Press.

# INTRODUCTION

Kids with Mum

Meadow Grove, Shirehampton is an English street of red brick houses constructed between the two World Wars. Built on the remains of an ancient apple orchard, the street became home to many Bristolian families, many of whom could trace their roots back to the beginnings of the village. One branch of our family, the Porters can be traced back to the 1500s through an inscription related to William Porter, one of the King's Boatmen, in an old prayer book kept in St. Mary's Church. So, we know at least one branch of our family was in the area 500 years ago. And, an Edyth Porter married one Richard Hardwick in Easton-in-Gordano, across the Avon from Shire, in the 1600s, so we know that the family was still thriving back then. My great-grandmother was also an Edyth Porter before marrying Great-Grampy Frank Saunders.

Shire, as we called the village, was my childhood home, my playground and my school. Our family consisted of Mum and Dad (Joyce and Ron Powell), my brother Alan and me, plus our many relatives, all who had roots in the village. Our oldest living relative was Great-Grampy Frank who was in his nineties and the youngest, at that time, was my brother Alan.

The village itself has an ancient history, dating back to Neolithic times and its name, Shirehampton, is thought to have originally meant the "dirty little homestead." Shire is situated on the River Avon, about three miles from the mouth of the Avon where it joins the Severn, and eight miles from Bristol City Centre. We moved to Meadow Grove when I was three years old in 1949, the year my brother Alan was born, and we stayed there until 1962, when we moved down to Dorset.

We had a difficult life: Dad had been a German prisoner-of-war for five years before he was demobilized and married Mum in 1945. He suffered from "bad nerves" as did many men who had fought in the war. The children came along very quickly and my first brother, Michael, died as a baby, when he was almost two. Money was short, the winters were cold, but we always had food on the table thanks to Mum's clever housekeeping. The street consisted of young couples with children, the Baby Boomers, and older families, some of whose sons and daughters had died during the war. Growing up, Alan and I had a lot of freedom to roam and we relied a lot on our imaginations and our companions.

This is the story of my childhood in Shirehampton during the 1950s.

# THE FAMILY

Nibley Road

Home in 1949 was one of fifty red-brick semi-detached houses on a street called Meadow Grove, Shirehampton. Before that, we lived on Nibley Road, a row of prefabricated, concrete houses built for the returning WWII servicemen and their families. The village of Shirehampton was often referred to as Shire by the locals or just the Village.

Meadow Grove was home to a bevy of young families, many with children our age: there was never any shortage of playmates. Life was tough. Dad worked at nearby Avonmouth for several industrial companies: the carbon black factory, the fertilizer plant, and the metal smelting works, to name a few. The jobs were dirty and the carcinogens that Dad worked with led to his eventual demise in his sixties. Mum worked evenings at the biscuit factory and helped clean other people's houses. There was always food on the table, and we grew most of our own vegetables in the back garden. But the houses were cold and damp with only a fireplace in the living room and no heating upstairs. In the winter we got dressed to go to bed and on winter mornings there were frost patterns on the insides of the window panes. We had a tough life, but we survived as did many families in similar post-war circumstances.

We enjoyed an extended family that was scattered around Bristol. Nana Win and Grampy Jim Powell, Dad's parents, lived in Shire in a house on Hung Road overlooking the Portway. Aunty Marge (Dad's oldest sister) and Uncle Arthur Paines lived up the road from them on Springfield Avenue with cousin David, who was the oldest grandchild of the clan. Aunty Mary (Dad's other sister) and Uncle Basil Hill, moved from Shire to Kingswood, where they raised our three cousins: Judith and Richard and, later, Katherine. On Mum's side, her parents Nana (Sylvia) and Grampy (Albert) Tanzell lived up in Broadmead, in a flat over a shop on the Mall. Aunty Alice, Mum's sister, married George Rollo and gave us our cousin George, who was my first boyfriend until our parents said cousins couldn't marry! Mum's youngest sister by 12 years, Aunty Sylvia later married Uncle Bob Gibbard and raised two of our littlest cousins: Linda and Dawn.

In addition, there were Great-Grandparents, numerous great aunts and uncles and many cousins multiple times removed. No walk around the village was complete without stopping off at a couple of relatives for a chat and a cup of tea. We didn't have much in the way of money, but this was made up for by a bevy of loving adults to fuss over us and plenty of cousins and friends to help us explore the local woods and fields around Shire, usually accompanied by our black and white mongrel dog, Spot.

# APPLE BLOSSOM

Apple Trees

Meadow Grove was built on the remains of an ancient apple orchard. These orchards, I believe, belonged to the private Norton Estate and provided apples for making "scrumpy" – a hard cider. Most gardens, on the Avonmouth side of the street, had one or two old apple trees that still bore good fruit each summer. Some of my earliest memories are of the apple trees in blossom. There is no smell sweeter or a sight more beautiful than apple blossom against a blue sky. When all the apple trees up and down the street were in blossom it was quite a sight. The trees seemed to cycle yearly: some years the blossom would be scant and the apples scarce. Other years the blossom would be profuse and the apples abundant. You never could tell what would happen from year to year. The trees produced an excellent, solid, green apple that was good for baking and eating. They were a little tart but, in a good year, would grow large and juicy and would keep for several months in a cold larder.

They were good climbing trees and my brother Alan and I would take cushions up into the branches and comics to read when the weather was warm. Dad threw ropes over the branches for swings that lasted until we wore out the ropes. Our cats loved to climb the trees, too, to chase the birds. We watched, one summer, as our small, black kitten stalked a bird out to the end of a branch. The bird flew, the kitten flew, and the kitten landed, unharmed but very surprised, in the grass beneath the tree.

Mum loved the apple trees and made good use of them. She would stew up apples with foraged blackberries to eat with warm custard, baked them with brown sugar and sultanas (large, plump raisins) in the cored middles, and made them into numerous apple pies. We never had a Sunday pork roast without Mum's own apple sauce. Some years we had so many apples that friends and relatives all got bags when they visited. Apples were also, of course, taken to Harvest Festival in the autumn. Despite eating them so often as a child, they became my favorite fruit.

The apple trees played a big part in our childhood games. They became the home base for games of hide and seek and they heard our counting from 1 to 100 so many times, it surprised me that the trees couldn't count too. They also heard "Cree, cree, cree, releaster", the ancient Celtic cry that we had got back before getting caught, so often it could have been etched into the tree's bark. The trees became pirate ships, desert islands, and look-outs. With no television in our house, we just had our imaginations to work with. Apples also became our weapon of choice in neighborhood battles, which raged from time to time with the neighboring Lloyd boys. "Fallers", apples that fell off the tree too early or too late and rotted, became squishy projectile that could be thrown at least two garden widths. Unfortunately, the trees were old and eventually produced fewer apples. Dad and Grampy Jim, decided to prune the trees. They did a severe pruning, thinking the trees would put out new growth, but the trees never came back to their full glory. It was a lesson in impermanence. Although the trees are no more, their legacy lives on in the name of the street, Meadow Grove.

# JOYCE

Mum as a young Housemaid

Mum's mum, Nana Tanzell, then Sylvia Rose Palmer, probably never went to school. Nana's family was "dirt poor" and lived in the slums of Bedminster, a very impoverished part of Bristol. Our Great-Granny was Maude Palmer, formerly a Hathaway, raised seven children on her own: we were told that Great-Grampy Palmer had left Bristol for Australia. The story went that Granny would or could not "cross water" so she stayed behind with the children. The truth, if it was ever told, was more likely that Grampy Palmer had been transported to the Colonies for some petty crime. But the truth is never fully told in some families. So, Granny Palmer took in washing and "made do and mend" to raise her fatherless brood.

In her teens, Sylvia (Sylv) was sent to work as a housemaid for a large Bristol family. There she met my charming grandfather, Albert (Alb) Tanzell, and they began a serious courtship. However, as some serious relationships go, she became pregnant. If the pregnancy had become known, she would have been fired instantly, so Sylv bound up her stomach so that the pregnancy would not show. As her time to deliver approached, Maude bundled her off to a Catholic Mother and Baby Home, where Sylv gave birth to Catherine Joyce, named after one of the nuns. Sylv returned to be a housemaid and Joycie stayed at the Home until she was almost two years old. Mum says that she can remember those times, remembers being sat in a highchair with a wool bonnet on because she banged her head. But these memories could have come from family stories. What was true was that Mum was loved by the nuns and given kind, loving care.

A continuation of the serious relationship with Alb resulted in another pregnancy for Sylv, and the birth of my Aunty Alice. Around this time Sylv and Alb married and brought Joycie home to live with them. Home was a series of damp basement flats with bug ridden beds. But Mum and Alice thrived despite Alb often being out of work, drunk, and no food in the pantry. Nana Tanzell had a hard life. She had to work as a housekeeper as Alb had a history of getting fired from almost every job he had. Joycie's birth didn't get registered until she was ten years old. Both Joycie and Alice went to a local school and stayed until fourteen years of age, when Joycie became a housemaid.

Nana Tanzell made sure that Joycie was employed by a decent Bristolian family who welcomed this bright, young woman. She worked hard: was up early to rake the stoves and clean shoes, until late when she cleaned the kitchen and banked the stoves for the night. She worked as a nursemaid to the children of the family, and walked the dogs, and in return was gifted with clothing, shoes, and many other things that her meager salary could not cover. Living in a large, warm, clean house was probably heaven to Joyce, as she was now known, despite the hard work. She stayed with the family as a maid until the outbreak of World War II. Joyce, now sixteen, returned to help Sylvia look after her new child, another Sylvia. By this time the Tanzells had moved to Shirehampton and this was where Joyce met her future husband, my Dad Ronald Powel

## GOT A KISS FOR ME?

Dad at the Docks

When Mum was sixteen, the family moved once again, to a redbrick Council house on Barrow Hill Crescent in Shirehampton. The houses overlooked an old red-clay quarry that had been used for centuries to make bricks and tiles. Mum was often required to stay home to look after her sisters and that's when she met Dad for the first time.

Mum was sixteen, Ron was three years older and reportedly shy, so it was a surprise that he should talk to her. As they were passing a group of boys "up the village", Joyce bent down to give her little sister Sylvia a kiss. Most of the boys laughed but Ron asked her if she had a kiss for him!

They started courting, as it was called back then, but the war intervened and Ron was sent off to Yeoville, Somerset, for training as a soldier. Before he was shipped off to France, Ron and Joyce became engaged to be married. Little did they know that they would have to wait five years before they saw each other again.

During the war, while waiting for Ron to return home, Joyce worked in a bakery, as a guard on the railway at Temple Meads Station, and even put out incendiary bombs on rooftops as a fire volunteer.

Ron's mum, Winifred Powell, spent the war years teaching Joyce to cook, knit and sew. They scrounged everything they could: thread, cloth, sugar, flour, and knitting wool to make necessities for the soldiers and airmen overseas. When the news came via the Red Cross that Ron had been taken as a Prisoner of War in Poland, Nana started sending Red Cross Parcels to him and other POWs.

Joyce was a strong-minded woman and waited out the intervening years, buying household items with her small wages and putting them aside for her eventual marriage. When she married, she had everything she needed to run a household: brushes and dusters, cutlery and china, tablecloths and bed linens. When Ron returned from the war in 1945, in poor health and with a history of his own, he and Joyce were married up in Bedminster. Ron's Mother had made all the arrangements and the marriage took place a few days after his arrival home.

After five years of waiting both Ron and Joyce had grown and changed and it was, perhaps, asking a lot of them to start married life after so long a separation. But they did and were lifelong partners. Life was not easy for them. The children came along very quickly and getting to know one another had to take place between nappy changing and baby feedings. Yet, they survived. Both were the descendants of a long line of West Country stock: tough, imaginative, and resourceful.

Ron got a job, first as an electricity meter reader, then a succession of jobs at Avonmouth docks and the factories on the Avonmouth industrial estate. He was a hard worker and a quick learner, but he had a restless soul and changed jobs when he felt that he could do better. Often, this was not for the better and he found himself, impatient again and wanting more change. It was not the jobs that were at fault. Dad had a high intelligence (he could compute complicated math in his head) and, under different circumstances could have become a mathematician or university professor. The war and returning home to family responsibilities created a different path for him. Who knows what he could have become given a different set of circumstances?

# A MISSING BROTHER

Prisoners of War (Dad in the Middle)

We were an ordinary family, but we had a secret. We had a missing brother. Dad had been called up to the Royal Corps of Signals during WWII, and was a dispatch rider, carrying messages between platoons on his motorbike. Unfortunately, he was captured in France by the Germans and his motor bike was squashed by a tank. He was made to march from camp to camp until he was interred as a Prisoner of War in Marionsberg, Poland. The farm-camp, Stalag XXB12, was his home from October 1942 until his release.

During the time that Dad was a Prisoner of War, Mum worked as a Railway Guard at Bristol Temple Meads train station, often accompanying trains, as most of the men were away at war. The ladies loaded the luggage and post into the guard van and made sure all the passengers were on board before blowing her whistle and waving the flag for departure. Many times, Mum had to accompany trains full of injured soldiers and occasionally one full of bodies in coffins that were being returned to their loved ones. Many soldiers were lost overseas or buried in foreign fields, but some made it home. It was a difficult time with different expectations. None of the soldiers knew if they would make it home alive.

Shortly after Mum and Dad were married, they heard, via the Red Cross, that a Russian girl that Ron had fallen in love with, at the farm, had given birth to a boy: Dad's son. Dad carried a poem by Patience Strong, "In the Heart of a Rose", in his wallet for many years as a remembrance of her. Dad referred to her as the "farmer's daughter".

Our family later heard that the girl had married and moved to Germany after the war ended. This fueled a great anger in Ron and during our childhood we could never mention anything German, and never have any toys that had been made in Germany. When baby Michael died, Dad entered a deep depression that he never quite got over. Mum was always worried that there would be a knock on the door and my Father would be taken away by the other woman and her son. Dad's parents and sisters all denied the existence of the child and claimed that, if known, this knowledge would have brought dishonor to the family, and that it was "just a tale". But I saw my Dad reading the poem in his wallet, saw the fear in my Mother's eyes, felt Dad's intense hatred of everything German, and knew there was more to the story than just a fiction. Somewhere, in Germany was a long-lost brother who probably didn't even know he had another family in England

# THE HEALTH CLINIC

I think that the reason that Alan and I grew up to be such strapping kids was partly due to the Shirehampton Health Clinic, down on St. Bernard's Road. We came from sturdy, country genes but after the war food and jobs were scarce. In 1946, the National Health Service was formed, and this provided free health service to every person in the UK. The British Government had also instituted rationing of food and clothes but there was always extra provision made for mothers and babies. At the Clinic Mum could obtain powdered milk to supplement bottled milk, and concentrated orange juice. There were no oranges to be had in England after the war, so the concentrate was a great luxury for any family. Along with vitamins, tonics, and remedies for everyday complaints we were perhaps one of the healthiest generations ever raised. We were measured, weighed and inspected in every way possible to ensure that we were growing up healthy. The Clinic also housed hearing, vision, and dental departments. By the age of eight, when my visual myopia (short-sightedness) became apparent, it was at the Clinic that I got my first pair of pink plastic, National Health Service glasses. I looked sort of goofy, but I could finally see!

The Clinic was a respite for young mums, at their "wits end" with crying babies. The little ones could be placed in a nursery play group during visits and the mums could have a few minutes to cry with the District Nurse. I think this did them more good than any modern therapy. There were other remedies for tired housewives. One day my Aunty Marge came down to our house on Meadow Grove, full of "vim and vinegar." Mum asked her why she was in such good spirits?

"Well, love, the doctor gave me these wonderful, little purple pills. They make the day go by so quickly and I get so much done, and I feel wonderful!" raved Marge.

She gave Mum some of the little, purple pills and Mum was soon whizzing through her housework too! Unfortunately, what the doctor had ordered for Marge were the early version of amphetamines, "Purple Bombers", and when Mum and Marge found out they flushed the pills down the toilet. No wonder they had so much energy!

We also had a doctors' office, The Surgery, in the village, up at the top of Lower High Street. Despite the bolstering of our wellbeing by the Health Clinic, we were frequent visitors with colds, flu and the "catarrh" in the winter and "wobbly tummy" in the summer. There was no refrigeration then except the new freezer at the Cooperative store. Our medical lives were documented in fat, little packets which were filed in a cubbyhole of an office just outside the doctors' offices. In addition to getting medical advice, tonics and remedies, the doctors' surgery was a place to swap gossip, proclaim on "how big" each other's children were getting and commiserate on more serious illnesses. Children were not innocent about illness and death. We knew when a child or adult had died on the street: when the ambulance men brought out a stretcher covered with a red blanket. Household curtains were kept drawn when someone died so you always treated the family with respect and consideration. Even as children we talked about the dead in hushed tones, learning early on the social mores that accompany death and dying.

# RATIONING

Rationing Post War

During the few years at the end and after the war families carried identity cards and had to use rationing books at the shops. Rationing of food and clothing had begun in 1939, was phased out in 1949, and ended for good on 4<sup>th</sup> July 1952. Mum kept our ration coupon books in the larder for many years longer "just in case." Medical records from that era showed that people were healthier during rationing than in later years when food was plentiful.

*Rations per Person per Week*
*2oz butter*
*4oz bacon or ham*
*4oz margarine*
*8oz sugar*
*Meat to a value of 1shilling and sixpence*
*2-3 pints milk*
*2oz cheese*
*1 fresh egg each week*
*2oz loose tea*
*1lb jam every two months*
*1 packet dried eggs every four weeks*
*12oz sweets every four weeks*

Meals were catered around these food rations and many ingenious recipes were thought up. For example, some jam companies began making preserves from colored apple puree with wooden pips to resemble strawberry jam. Some families processed acorns to make a coffee substitute.

People were encouraged to "Dig for Victory" and most families had a vegetable garden, an allotment of land where they could grow fruits and vegetables or keep chickens for fresh eggs or rabbits for meat. Other items on ration were rice and dried fruit, tinned goods, flour, treacle, syrup, jellies, and mincemeat, biscuits, and soap. Coal, gas and electricity were also rationed. Clothing was rationed with a point system that allowed people to buy some new clothing but most people "made do and mended."

Many women took to cutting up older clothes to make new creations by adding braids and fancy stitch work. Others patiently unraveled outworn, woolen sweaters to knit up into new ones. Darning wool was even carefully unwound and knitted up into new scarves, gloves and socks.

Even after the war, school girls were given lessons in how to darn socks, patch sheets, hem dresses, embroider, smock, and how to "turn a sheet". Turning a sheet meant cutting a worn sheet down the middle, joining the two good sides together with a flat seam down the middle and hemming the worn parts into new side seams. This way a worn sheet could last a few more years.

Most girls, by the time they were ten years old, could knit, crochet, embroider and, perhaps, even tat, which meant making a type of lace for edging sheets and pillow cases. Clothing, that had some life, was remade into new clothes and clothes too old for anything were made into cleaning rags. Nothing was wasted. Recycling was the norm. The motto of that time was "waste not, want not!"

# GREAT-GRAMPY FRANK

Great-Grampy Frank, Alan and Angela

The first memories I have of Great-Grampy Frank Saunders are at the market town of Frome, in the Somerset countryside. He was living at the time with one of his daughters, Aunty Kath and Uncle Ben on New Street, which was actually a very old row of country cottages. It was summer time and the back garden was a riot of pink, gold, and orange: petunias, marigolds, and nasturtiums. Around five years old, I was an active, happy child, always dancing and skipping and I was dancing for Great-Grampy Frank.

In between dancing I would pick flowers for him, laying them in his blanketed lap, as he sat outside in the warm sunshine. Aunty Kath's "budgie", a little blue and yellow bird, was out too and sang along with me. Frank would have turned ninety and while deaf, loved his "babbies", as he called us.

His wrinkled hands gathered the delicious flowers into a bunch to smell and I picked more and more. I stayed away from the end of the garden where a steep climb could be made, by ladder, down to the River Frome that ran through grazing meadows below. It was rumored that

Uncle Ben, who worked at the local brass foundry, had buried a cache of brass ornament there: I have often wondered if anybody ever dug them up and wondered where they came from?

Great-Grampy Frank's people were farming folk, the Saunders, who came from Bratton in Wiltshire. Today the countryside is famous for its flourishing wheat fields, its ancient horses cut into the white, clay hillsides, and anomalous crop circles that seem to appear out of nowhere. Close by is Salisbury Plain with its famous, standing, stone circles, mysterious Silbury Hill, Avebury's standing stones, and prehistoric burial tombs. I wonder if Great-Grampy's ancestors were living there when all this magic began?

Frank had worked at the docks for almost his whole life. He was a short, extremely strong man in his youth and rumored to be able to pull a locomotive along the tracks. He raised a family of strongly independent children at Avonmouth and I remember him as a kindly, blue-eyed gent who always had a kind word and a sixpenny piece from his pension money for his "babbies." His wife, Edyth (a former Porter from Easton-in-Gordano, across the river from Shire) was a strong-minded woman. She took in washing from the boats docked at Avonmouth, was a staunch member of her Methodist church, and even volunteered in the early suffragette movement! She was not your typical wife and mother, but fiercely independent and the ruler of her household. She passed away shortly after I was born so I never had the privilege of knowing her as a person. Her daughters helped her with the laundry and her sons went to work at the docks like their father. Frank and Edyth were together more than sixty years and now rest together in Shirehampton Cemetery.

# AFTER THE BLITZ

Blitzed Church

During the war Bristol was badly "blitzed", meaning that many of its historic buildings and many family homes were bombed. The British and Americans did their share of bombing, too, with the result that many, beautiful German cities like Dresden were reduced to rubble. After the war, Bristol underwent a period of rebuilding with modern buildings like the Lewis's and Debenham's boat-like structure and the Cooperative's Fairfax store.

As a little girl, I remember some buildings open to their basements: colorful wild flowers beautifying their stark devastation. Not having lived through the Blitz, the bombed-out buildings did not have a great deal of meaning to me except that many families had lost their homes. Aunty Marge told us that she was bombed out of three houses in Shire and had to set up a new home each time!

Some good came from the bombing as old slums made way for new shopping centers and housing estates. The estates were meant to be a new way of living, but some slum families kept their coal in the bathtub! One family even caught ducks from a local pond and made use of their bathtub as a make-do, indoor pond. The old slums did not have indoor plumbing and many families didn't know what to do with it. As an example, Nana Tanzell told us that her family wore their underwear all winter and only changed it when the weather turned warm. It took many years for the slum families to adjust to the post-war concepts of personal hygiene.

Some interesting discoveries were made, too, when clearing away the bombed-out buildings. At a site close to the new Lewis's store, construction workers unearthed what they called an old "plague pit." During the 1600s the bubonic plague had killed around three-quarters of the European population. The plague was carried in by rats off the ships in the docks. Because of the lack of burial plots, and people to bury them, bodies were placed in multiple graves.

It brought home to us how much 20th century Bristolians were survivors of this disease and many other plagues like Scarlet Fever, Diphtheria, and Tuberculosis. Interestingly, many children's songs served as an oral history of those times. Nursery rhymes such as Ring-a-Ring-O'Roses, was an example. Rosaries or prayer beads were carried to prevent disease and citizens also carried posies of herbs and scented flowers to ward off the smell. Sneezing was one of the symptoms of the disease as were circles of boils, the "rings of roses". Corpses were frequently burned, hence the "ashes" and most people succumbed to the disease, thus the "falling down" in the rhyme.

We were a hardy generation, the post-war Bristol kids. We braved the cold winters, freezing bedrooms, rationing, and no refrigeration. In summer, most foods were dumped in vinegar to preserve them, a condiment I despise to this day. Canned salmon, cucumber, or beetroot, all were vinegar soused by Mum so that they could last a few more days. The modern houses, that replaced the bombed-out buildings, now had pantries and larders and meat safes, and some of the newer, prefabricated buildings even had fridges, quite an advancement for a new age.

# THE WORKING CLASSES

Slum Children (* My Mum and her younger sister)

Following the war there was a reshuffling of the British class system. Prior to WWII, there was a definite class system ranging from the dissolute poor, up through the working and middle classes, and on up to the aristocracy. Men and women in each class understood their roles and stations. Apart from being wives and mothers there were very few working opportunities for women of any class.

During the war, with so many men abroad, women found themselves doing jobs, that men took for granted. Women worked in munitions factories, drove buses, or, like my mother, worked as railway guards and porters. Not only did this give them a working salary and spending money, but it gave them a status outside the home. When the war ended, in 1945, women reluctantly returned to their homes, giving up their jobs to the returning servicemen.

However, women had tasted freedom and income and the beginning of women's working independence had started. Women had the vote, and now they had the opportunity to work outside the home. New opportunities however, passed Mum by. Now, having a young family, she went back to cleaning houses. Sometimes I went with her. One day, when I was about ten years old, I found myself cleaning the playhouse of the daughters of the residence. Even at that young age, I realized what I was doing and vowed that I would not clean houses for a living, like my

Mum. I loved her dearly but saw what she had given up. When she talked about her adventures on the railway, she had a lift in her voice and a light in her eye. Cleaning other people's houses exhausted her physically, emotionally, and spiritually.

The class system also had its reverse snobbery. Not only did the middle and upper classes look down on the working ranks but the working classes sneered at the middle classes. There were even levels of lower, middle and upper working classes that all sneered at each other! Dad's younger sister had decided to train as a nurse, during the war, and became a nursing sister at the Bristol Royal Infirmary. She was now considered "above herself" and a "snob", by the rest of the family because she took daily baths instead of once a week, dropped her Bristolian slang, and dressed nicely. She was considered to have deserted her working-class roots.

When I turned seventeen, I decided that I would like to train as a nurse, too, and had to appease my angry mother who thought that I would reject her and our family, once I became a nurse. It took me a year before I could summon up the courage to face my mother. Not only was I defying centuries of working-class norms but also depriving the family of my income, as I decided to live in the nurses' residence. Young women were expected to give their wages to their mothers, in those days, and receive an allowance for stockings and other personal effects. Later, deciding to go to college was yet another great adventure in class expectations!

# ALAN, THE EXPLORER

My Brother Alan

My younger brother Alan should have grown up to be an explorer, a discoverer of new things, an adventurer on a level with Indiana Jones. Perhaps if he had been born into a different social class, he would have climbed Everest, found a cure for cancer, or become a great civic leader. However, being born into a British, working class family, great expectations were not the norm. Youngsters were expected to carry on the working traditions of the family. For me, that would have been to work in a factory, or an office worker, then raise a family, and, for Alan, to work at the docks or some other service-related job.

Alan had a decidedly adventurous nature: he knew no fear! A neighbor once came over to tell us that young Alan was climbing out of his bedroom window, then reaching over and climbing in our parents' bedroom window. He would run around to his own bedroom and repeat the same tricky exercise. He was always finding boarded-up cottages, houses, and grander mansions where he would climb in and investigate. I once joined him on one of his adventures and we explored one of the old cottages to the side of the Rising Sun pub up in the village. It was spooky inside but exciting. I was more worried about getting caught than Alan, but he brought out my adventurous side.

With his high intelligence, great language skills, and sense of exploration, Alan was always setting off on some quest. Many times, I went along with him and sometimes he took some of the boys from the primary school. Most times he came back on his own and now and again Mum and Dad would have to send the police out to find him. Often, we would never know where he was!

The education system of that time did not help either. Primary school was great as, post war, we were part of the Baby Boom and educational experimentation was the fashion. However, the secondary schools were still in a rut, teaching the three R's and turning out working class replicas. Girls learned how to cook, sew, and use a typewriter: boys learned to do wood and metal work, and fix a car. Alan had a great eye for detail and his technical drawing skills could have set him on a path towards a career as a draftsman or architect. However, he left school with his ambition squashed out of him. The thinking was, why educate children beyond what society expects of them. It took a decidedly rebellious child and a very supportive school to transcend that tradition.

## MOTHERING SUNDAY

Mother's Day was not invented by the greeting card companies as some would have us believe. It was originally Mothering Sunday which took place on the fourth Sunday of Lent. Mothering Sunday was an ancient custom in England dating back to the days when many young girls, some as young as ten years old, were put to work as maids in the Big Houses owned by moneyed families. Mothering Sunday was the day that these young girls were given a day off to visit their mothers and their families. Servants had very little free time off in those days.

The origins of Mothering Sunday also come from church history when it was thought to be important for people to visit their "Mother" church, usually a cathedral in the city, once a year. "Mother" churches had "Daughter" churches in outlying villages, which many people attended. Mothering Sunday usually took place at the end of Lent and scattered families came together to celebrate this special day. The custom may have had an earlier origin from pagan times where goddess worship was prevalent.

The early English custom was that children, usually daughters, would pick wildflower posies which they would take to the church and give to their mothers. Girls also baked a traditional cake for their mothers called Simnel Cake: a rich, fruit cake covered with sweet, almond paste, which also celebrated the end of the Lenten fast. The origins of this cake are said to reach back to Roman times and was originally made with flour, spices, and studded with dried nuts and candied fruit peel. Simnel cakes were traditionally decorated with eleven small balls of almond paste to represent all the Apostles, except Judas.

In Shire, this custom had lost most of its historic importance and Mothering Sunday at the Baptist Church was a service of recognition for mothers. The children were asked to invite their mothers to Sunday School and to bring small bunches of flowers, including traditional violets, which were presented to the mothers. Nana Win's garden was raided for small flowers like lobelia and tiny, pink rosebuds which, with Nana's help we made into posies. As we got older, violets, primroses, and wood anemones from Shirehampton golf course woods were eagerly picked and used for posies instead of garden flowers.

At Sunday School special hymns were sung by the children in praise of mothers such as *All Things Bright and Beautiful* and *Give, Said the Little Flower*, to recognize that our mothers were always giving to us. The Cradle Rolls, records of new baby births, were brought out and all the new babies that had been "Dedicated" in the church were recognized. After Sunday School we would visit Nana Win in Shire or catch the bus up to Bristol to visit with Nana Tanzell. Nana Tanzell didn't like flowers very much, so we would usually take her a box of Turkish Delight, a rosewater scented confection, that she would share with us. But, like most kids, the next day we forgot to honor our mother, and were back to taking her for granted. She cooked and cleaned for us, washed our clothes and dirty faces, and loved us. At least one day out of the year we would remember to show our appreciation!

# THE "CHARABANG" TO WESTON SANDS

Playing at Weston Sands

Every year Shirehampton Baptist Church arranged a trip for the Sunday School children to Weston-Super-Mare beach. The trip to Weston was eagerly anticipated, buckets and spades were brought out from the cupboard-under-the-stairs, and swimming costumes located. We would assemble outside the Savoy Cinema early in the morning with our mums and dads. The "charabang", (that's how we pronounced it) a large, square bus, would eventually pull up and we would all pile in. Off we would go, laughing and joking, only to pull up half an hour later so all the kids who were feeling sick, including me, could get out and throw up on the grass verge. After that we all felt better and couldn't wait to get to the Weston sands.

Soon the wide Promenade of the seafront would come into view and we would be dropped off for the short walk to pick a spot on the beach. Off came our shoes as we scuffled along the sandy, concrete esplanade, eying the ice cream stands that we would visit later. One of our favorite places was the donkey rides. When the tide was well out, there was a huge, flat expanse of sand along which wagons were pulled by ponies. I loved the uncomplaining donkeys, standing patiently in a group, waiting for a child to come up and choose one for a ride. Each donkey had their name stenciled on a leather band above their nose: Bluebell, Snowy, Patch, and many others. There was a good, long ride up and down the beach which gave rise to a famous Bristol saying: "Up and down like a Weston donkey."

While we were riding the donkeys, Mum and Dad would have rented a couple of deck chairs and set up a camp close by with bags, towels, buckets and spades. Some people had canvas wind-breakers on poles but we braved the stinging sand in windy weather. At this point the tide wouldn't be too far out so we quickly changed under towels into our swimming costumes and grabbed our buckets and spades. Dad would tie a large white handkerchief into a four-pointed sun-hat, to cover his balding spot, and settle down for a quick nap in his deck chair. Mum would tuck up her skirts and with bare feet chase with us down to the waves. The water was usually quite cold, so we satisfied ourselves with wading and splashing before becoming architects, building castles in the wet sand. Decorating the castles with shells and small paper flags, we vied to see who could build the highest stronghold. In a macabre dance, we would then jump on top of our castles singing "I'm the king of the castle and you're a dirty rascal!" In an even stranger ritual, we would then start digging holes, as deep as we could, and we would then jump in and out of these holes. There was probably some vestige of ancient memory working somewhere in our childish minds to build and then destroy these castles and turn them into holes!

Sometime during the day Alan would go missing, he loved to explore, but we knew where to find him. After walking up and down the beach calling his name, we would visit the First Aid Hut and there would be Alan, wrapped in a blanket, sipping hot cocoa. "Where have you been?" he would ask "I've been waiting for you!"

All this activity got us hungry and we would gather up Alan and our belongings and troop up to the fish and chip shop for fried cod and chips and hot tea to warm us up. We would laugh at the naughty postcards on display at every souvenir shop along the Front and then make our way to the pier. At the entrance we gorged ourselves on sweet, pink sticks of seaside rock with Weston imprinted all the way through, fluffy candy floss, and Cornish ice cream in square cornets. We printed out our names on small metal strips, had our fortunes and weights guessed, and tried to pick up soft toys with mechanical cranes.

Electric trains ran up and down the length of the pier, but we preferred to walk, it was more exciting. Our destination was the funfair at the end of the pier where we spent the better part of the afternoon enjoying the rides: the roller coaster, the ghost train and the merry-go-round.

Soon, it was time to find our way back to the "charabang" to load our sandy, sugar-sticky selves back on board. There was much stowing of bags and buckets and crying from tired, little children. There was no travel sickness on the ride back home as most of us fell asleep soon after the bus began its journey home to Shirehampton.

## THE RIVER BANK

The Avon, referred to as the River Avon or just The River, meanders past the village of Shirehampton in a straight line until it reaches the Horseshoe Bend. Here it takes a wide loop befitting its name, before it continues to the city of Bristol and the old docks. Starting at Avonmouth, where the salty tide flows in from the Severn Channel, the Avon is a muddy river that fills up to its grassy banks at its fullest tide, then empties to a trickle between deep, mud banks at its lowest. Over a hundred years ago great sailing ships came up and down the river taking advantage of the two, forty-foot, daily tides that replenish the river.

Many kings stopped off at Shirehampton, where the "river rats", pilots from Pill, would then lead the boats safely up to the Bristol Docks. One of my ancestors, William Porter in the 1500's, was one of the King's boatmen. In 1877, a new dock was opened at Avonmouth, and the number of boats coming up the river diminished. My Great-Grandfather, Grandfathers, my Dad, and multiple Uncles all worked at the Bristol and Avonmouth docks.

Each year, we would troop down to the river bank to watch the Severn Bore, a spring tidal wave that would race up the river, sometimes causing flooding if it came up over the banks. It was exciting to watch this wall of water, sometimes several feet high, race silently up the river. There was a thrill to watching this mysterious event, which our ancestors must have also watched, with existential awe.

To us, the river bank was a playground. Wild flowers grew lavishly on its abandoned banks including wild mustard, mallow; ox-eye daisies; the six-foot, yellow spears of solitary mullein; wild parsnip; common vetch; rosebay willow herb; and ladies bedstraw, to name a few. The sewers dumped into the stretch of the river adjoining the lower Portway, so other, not-so-nice, things could be seen floating in the rising tidal waters. The river had its own smell: rancid mud at low tide and a salty tang at high tide. We could always tell when the tide was out in summer, even across the other side of the village the smell was rank! River rats, red foxes, and badgers had homes on the river banks but we usually only knew they were there by their tracks in the soft mud.

One summer the Lloyd brothers decided to see if they could cross the river at low tide. I remember them up to their knees in soft mud as they labored back to the Shire side of the river. They resembled mud-men as they climbed up the banks, the green-grey mud drying on their skin. They smelled to "high heaven' and we wondered what their Mum would have to say when they reached home. Amazingly, none of us ever got sick from playing near the river but an outbreak of poliomyelitis in the mid-1950s put an end to us going near the sewers. Eventually, many of the Shire children received some of the first Salk vaccines for polio and we were safe from this crippling disease.

An evening walk along the river bank, with Mum and Dad, Alan and me, with our dog Spot, often took us past the Lamplighters pub where Grampy Jim could be found enjoying a beer and a game of cards with his mates. Mum and Dad would stop so we could have lemonade and crisps in the riverbank garden adjoining the pub. In front of the Lamplighters was the kiosk for the Ferry that made frequent trips across the river, at high tide, to the village of Pill and back. On higher land near the ferry were the wooden carcasses of old sailing ships. We would pretend that we were sailors navigating the high seas and had many imaginative adventures. Even if we were not actual sailors, being Shire kids, we had salt water in our veins.

## THE FERRY OVER TO PILL

As soon as the weather turned warm Mum would take us on the ferry over to Pill, a small village on the other side of the River Avon. Taking a trip over to Pill on the small ferry boat was both wonderful and terrible at the same time. I was always afraid of the rushing, dirty-brown water and the slimy, grey-green mud that seemed to reach up and grab for my ankles. I would inch myself back on the cobblestone slipway and tried not to let the dirty, river water splash my summer sandals. To get there we would have walked down the river bank to the Lamplighters pub and paid our pennies at the metal toll-booth on the Shire side of the Avon. The short walk onto the cobblestone slipway was nerve-racking with its treacherous, slippery mud and the fast-flowing water reaching ever higher as the tide came in.

Across the river we would see the ferry boat pushing off from the Pill slipway. Bicycles would be secured in the prow and the wooden walkway would be hoisted aboard just behind the bikes. There were always several people in the boat: the boatman Sam Porter, one of our many distant relatives, Richard, his son who helped load and unload the gangplank, and the trusting passengers. The boat pushed off from the mud where it had been beached on the Pill side and Sam would gun the engine to get a start against the tide. The boat would push off in a wide arc that took the ferry boat against the tide until the boat was midstream, Sam would then let out the engine to allow the boat to come close to the Shire slip. With a final gun of the motor he would shove the boat up the side of the slipway, the prow biting a deep groove into the grey mud. There was a bustle of activity as the gangplank was noisily cantilevered across and onto the slipway and the passengers clomped heavily onto dry land. I always wondered how they could do it so easily and fearlessly.

Soon everyone on the Shire side boarded the ferry and we took our seats in the well of the boat. This was the exciting part—I felt safe here and protected from the wind and water.

On most trips we would take our dog Spot, a black and white wirehaired mongrel, with us on the ferry. This was another harrowing part of the ferry ride. Spot always jumped off the boat about halfway over and swam to the slipway on the Pill side. He seemed to enjoy battling the fast current and waited for us with wagging tail and tongue lolling out in a crazy grin. I was sure that one day he would drown but he never did.

From here we would walk up through the village of Pill, looking at the abandoned, wooden, sailing ships in the small, muddy harbor, stopping at the local off-license for lemonade and crisps with some other Porter relatives, before making our way up to the fields. Our walk would take us through cow pastures, lanes and woods where we would pick bunches of delicate, white, wood anemones and purple violets, along with primroses and yellow, spring celandines. Our destination was the reservoir, where Spot would take another swim and we would sit to eat our jam sandwiches. They were usually dried out from being wrapped in a brown, paper bag but we didn't care. We were hungry and we felt good from our walk in the fresh air. The Pill side was pretty much like the Shire side of the river, but we felt like explorers visiting a foreign land every time we took a ride over on the Pill ferry.

# PENPOLE AND KINGSWESTON

View from Penpole Point over Avon

As children Alan and I had a great deal of freedom to wander the neighborhoods around Shirehampton and we had several favorite hikes. Our usual trek was up Lower High Street, then up to Penpole Point. We climbed up the steep, grassy hill to the top of Penpole and from there had an excellent view out over the Severn Estuary and over to Wales. To our right lay Kingsweston Housing Estate, a rock quarry, and further views of the Severn Estuary. Some of the braver kids, including Alan, regularly climbed the quarry. I did it once, with my heart in my mouth, and vowed never to do it again. It was not an easy climb.

Up on top of Penpole was a long grassy ridge where once the ladies and gentlemen of historic Kingsweston House "took the air" before retiring to the Belvedere Tea House at the entrance to Kingsweston Woods. During the war the iron gates had been removed and the tea house and the stone walls were now in ruins, which was sad. They would later be demolished.

Once inside the woods, we would follow the dimly lit, woodsy–smelling paths, through firs and deciduous trees, which had been planted by Squire Miles back in the 1800s, until we emerged into the manicured lawns and grounds of Kingsweston House. This stately house had been built in the 1700s and had magnificent vistas out over the Severn and, on good days, views of the Welsh hills. During our childhood, everything was overgrown and brambly. What remained in the grounds was very mysterious to us. There were stone blocks that had been used to mount hunting horses, the vestiges of building foundations, a dilapidated laundry house, rubble-filled fishponds and several faux temples. All these sparked our imaginations.

Kingsweston House had been used as a private school but was boarded up and elusive during our visits. There were dreams I had, when I was young, of high, blue walls covered with paintings of famous people, which I later discovered were true. One summer Alan and I spent most of our school holidays cleaning up one of the faux temples, as roof tiles and plaster had fallen in. A column, on which a goddess statue once stood, was cleaned up and we found the sculpture locked in a gardener's hut. We brought brushes and dustpans and cleared as much of the temple as we could even though we did not know its true history.

From Kingsweston House we would trudge along to the House in the Garden, a Dower House, which later became a Special Education school. Here we would fish for tadpoles in the large fish pond that faced the road. Leaning over the stone wall we would lower jam jars tied with string to see what we could catch. In the summer there would be bluebells everywhere and we would pick armfuls to take home to Mum, who loved wild flowers.

If we kept on along the road, we came to the climb up through Dingle Dell woods where the bluebells grew so thick you couldn't see the ground. Climbing the path up through the woods we would come out again on a high ridge of land but this time we would be overlooking the River Avon and fields on the Somerset side of the Avon.

The ridge was ancient land covered with Iron Age barrows and earthworks. When we were little, the bumps and lumps in the grass just meant great places for running up and down. Later, when we understood the historic past of the site, we treated it with more respect. We could understand its strategic importance to the ancient peoples. It had extended views over the river and the estuary and all the land in between. There would have been wooden enclosures with huts, dogs, fires, people and daily life that we could only guess at.

## THE GOLF COURSE

Part of our roaming territory was Shirehampton Park and the golf course. The land used to belong to Squire Miles and, before that, the Norton Family, but it had been taken into safe keeping by the National Trust. We had to be aware of the golfers, but they were also wary of us and frequent cries of "Fore! Get off the bloody course!" would get us out of their way. On the Avon side, the land sloped steeply down to the Portway: a grassy, rocky hillside that I once fell down. I was picking wildflowers, lost my footing, and rolled to the bottom. I prayed to God to keep me safe and landed with just a few bruises. I got a ride home in a passing car, but poor Alan had to walk home, laden down with our coats. He stopped at each relative's house on the way home telling them that "Angela fell down the hill onto the Portway and a man in a car took her away!" We had relatives coming around all day thinking I had been lost forever!

On the Shire side the golf course bordered Shirehampton Road with its huge elms that eventually succumbed to Dutch Elm disease. There were also wonderful horse chestnut trees. These trees were, and still are, glories! In spring they unfurl large, pale green, banners of leaves and stacked plumes of pinkish flowers on their ample branches. By the autumn, as the foliage is crisping from green to brown, they display their horse chestnuts. The large, shiny mahogany-brown nuts are hidden in thick, prickly, green cases that split open when they hit the ground. Horse chestnuts are not good to eat but they make a wonderful weapon! We would collect the seeds and, while they were soft, Dad would bore a hole through them with a meat skewer. He would hide a few to harden for the next season. Dad would thread the others onto thick strings.

A *conker* on a string was then used in a play battle where each person tried to hit and break the other kid's *conker*. Historically, the games were played with shells on a string. If the *conker* was a good one (or saved from last year) they could become a "sixer", meaning that it had defeated six other *conkers*. Kids had different strategies, but it seemed that the shorter the hitting *conker*'s string, the better leverage you had to defeat your opponent. However, a shorter string also guaranteed a few sore knuckles!

In the middle of the golf course was a broad valley, or *coombe*, bordered by woodland. In the spring the woods were carpeted with primroses, violets and wood anemones, and, in one special place, we were able to pick cowslips. We didn't know it but these fragile, yellow, bell flowers were becoming scarcer and scarcer. Also, near the woods was a pond, where we could fish for tadpoles and sticklebacks, red and blue fish with spiny backs. The water for this pond originated in a spring on top of Penpole which made its way, eventually, out to the Avon.

Well-hidden was a venerable well, the Bucklewell. This ancient spring was said to have been around since Neolithic days and had healing properties for eye problems. It was called the Buckle Well because it flowed out from an outcropping of stone and visitors had to bend down to see into it. There is a history that there were the remains of a Roman altar at the site. We searched for this well, when we were children, but never found it because it had been bricked up before the Second World War. Eventually, the pond on the golf course was also filled in and covered over. Like so many traditional places around Shirehampton, history gave way to economy and convenience.

## ANCIENT REMAINS

The British Isles have an ancient and respected history and, as children, we were taken to visit many historical sites. In the 1950s Stonehenge was open to the public and during the summer Dad would load us in the sidecar, Mum would climb on the pillion of Dad's motorbike, and off we would go to Salisbury Plain. Many families would gather there in the summer months and there was always a van selling tea on the road near the ruins. No rules were imposed, and we were free to explore the stones, climbing on the fallen Bluestones and playing Touch around the standing Sarsens. Mum and Dad would try to interest us in the historic importance of the stones, but it wasn't until we were much older that the significance of the site had any meaning.

We took trips, too, out to Wiltshire, birthplace of Great-Grampy Frank, climbed Glastonbury Tor, drank the Chalice waters, danced around the standing stones at Avebury, climbed mysterious Clay Hill and Silbury Hill, and marveled at the beauty of the White Horses cut into the Wiltshire hillsides. Perhaps some of the old magic rubbed off on Alan and me because we both turned out to be very intuitive and able to have spontaneous Out-Of-Body Experiences from early childhood.

There were historic sites nearby too. Just outside of Bristol was another group of standing stones, at Stanton Drew, where Grampy Jim's parents the Powells, had farmed the land. In Shire itself, up on Penpole, a ridge of land rising above the village, were the remains of an Iron Age encampment with raised earthworks. And further down, close to Lower High Street, were the remains of a Roman Villa complete with underground hypocausts and a beautiful, tiled floor. We would play "Hide and Seek" under the stacked-stone vents and skip on the paved floor, until the local City Council fenced in the historic site. We were immersed in history, but we weren't aware of it until we were older. Then we were able to appreciate the age and meaning of our playgrounds.

## SATURDAY FILMS AT THE SAVOY

On Saturday mornings we would get our pocket money which started at a "thrupenny bit" (three penny piece) when we were little and made its way up to two shillings and sixpence in our teens. Out of this we bought sweets, purchased presents for relatives and, of course, paid to get in to the Saturday Pictures at the Savoy Cinema. The Savoy operated on Station Road between the Old School and the Public Hall. On Saturday's kids could be seen lining up to pay their money and get good seats. The Balcony was nine pence and the Stalls a "tanner" (sixpence). Before going into the theatre, we would buy lots of cheap sweets. Sugar rationing had ended in 1953 so there was plenty to choose from such as Rowntrees Fruit Pastilles, Jelly Babies and Chocolate Buttons. We could only afford the stalls which meant that rowdy kids in the balcony could throw food and drink, and even spit, down on us. The children who attended the matinees were a very noisy lot and it took several ushers with battery torches to calm us all down. The manager wouldn't start the films until everyone was quiet.

The matinees usually started with cartoons: Woody Woodpecker and various Disney cartoons featuring Pluto and Donald Duck, were regulars. He would respond to the Woodpecker movies by echoing his silly laugh, "Ha,ha,ha,ha,ha, hahahahahahahah!" After the cartoons the films would move on to the serials: The Little Rascals got up to their antics, Tarzan rescued Jane, and science fiction classics scared us enough to hunker down in our seats. If the audience became too boisterous, the manager would turn off the projector until we all quieted down again. Sometimes the celluloid film would break in the projector and "all hell" would break loose! This would persist until the manager fixed the reel and the ushers got us quiet again.

A few times, the manager, a resourceful man, attempted to keep us quiet until the films started, by staging a talent show. There would be a prize for the best act. In those days I was very quiet and shy, but I put up my hand as I knew all the words to Doris Day's song *Que Serra Serra*. We all trooped up on stage and formed a line. It must have been winter because I remember wearing a white, knitted hat. The children stood in front of the screen and, one by one, either recited or sang their pieces.

The audience, all local kids, was supposed to cheer and clap for their favorites but there was plenty of booing and hissing from the balcony. How I wished that I had never put up my hand! Eventually, it came to my turn and in my little girl, undeveloped voice sang the verses to *Que Serra Serra*. To give them their due, the audience did stay quiet during my song but there were as many boos as cheers at the end. I didn't win and left the stage with a very red face. I think they just didn't appreciate good music.

After a few years, the Savoy matinees were cancelled, and the Savoy became a bingo hall. Alan and I caught the bus up to the Orpheus in Henleaze where children's Saturday films were still being shown. Eventually when I started attending Portway Secondary School, I had to go up to Bristol for cello lessons on Saturdays, so stopped going to the matinees. As a family we still went to the evening pictures and saw all the Disney films, including The Living Desert, little knowing that one day I would be living and working in the Nevada desert.

# BIRTHDAYS

Birthdays were a big thing when we were children. Not the expensive, celebrity parties at pizza warehouses that children expect today but good, honest food with children, and even adults, invited. There was special food, party games, presents, and lots of fun. A typical party began with presents in the morning, if it was a weekend. If it was a school day, the presents might be kept until the child came home from school, to be opened with the whole family. Sometimes a party would be delayed until the weekend so that family members could come, particularly for a little child's party. The food was not fancy, and we always knew what to expect. Favorites were trifle, sausage rolls, and cheese straws. There were usually small sandwiches, with the crusts cut off, as it was a special occasion. Fairy cakes were also popular: little cakes baked in paper cases with icing on top. And there was always sliced bread and butter and jam. Following this would be canned fruit, such as sliced peaches, served with evaporated milk, along with several different jellies and a sweet, flavored, cornstarch mold called blancmange. Mum used a rabbit mold to make this pudding which would be turned out, when cold, onto a plate of green jelly.

Jelly was made the English way with blocks of concentrated, rubbery, jelly squares stirred into a measure of hot water until they melted. The jelly was left to cool, and then poured into a bowl or mold to set. A party without jelly was not a party! If the celebration was a fancy one, then *savories* such as Scotch eggs, and cocktail sausages on toothpicks would be prepared and served cold.

Every party culminated in the arrival of the birthday cake, topped with an exact number of candles for the child's age. As in other countries, the child would blow out the candles and make a wish. If the child was older, other children and adults would "bump" the birthday person.

Partiers would take hold of the arms and legs of the birthday boy or girl and gently bump them on the floor, the number matching their new age. Sometimes with older children and teenagers this could get quite rough!

Fancy paper hats would be saved from Christmas and come out of storage for birthday parties. Each child would be bedecked with a colored, crepe paper crown. Colorful, crepe paper would have been used for the room decorations, as well. Great imagination and creativity went into decorations. Party games came after the food: Pass the Parcel, Blind Man's Bluff, Pin the Tail on the Donkey: anything to create noise, laughter, and merriment. The organized parties that children experience today are tame compared to the parties we celebrated. The emotions were genuine, and most partygoers had a good time—except for the time I asked for an extra piece of cake!

    I went to a school friend's birthday party and, looking back at it now, the family must have had very little money. All the party food was there but in very small amounts. When it came time to cut the cake, we were given a tiny slice, small enough for a mouse. We soon got to playing games and I decided to ask my friend's mother for another piece of cake "for my brother." Unfortunately, I decided to eat the piece of cake during the party and was my face red, when I was caught! That was one party that I wanted to forget forever.

# THE SWIMMING POOL

The sound of a sports whistle transports me back to Shirehampton Swimming Baths and I break out in a rash of goose bumps, not from excitement but from memories of dressing in the chilly, changing rooms. My first memory of the baths was when we were taken from Avon Primary school for our first lesson. Getting changed was a challenge. You would try to keep the canvas curtain to your cubicle from flying open in the cold breeze, balance on the slatted, wooden mat and not get your feet on the chilly floor, and then rush through the icy cold, foot bath before you even reached the pool area.

There was a very jovial, older man who gave us our first lesson. We all sat on the edge of the shallow pool and he asked us "Do you see any goldfish?" We all chorused "No!" "Do you see any big fishes?" Again, we called out "No!" "Do you see any sharks?" Some of us squealed but the answer came back "No!" "Well, get in the water" he yelled. And we all plopped in like so many little, fat seals.

I was a very cautious swimmer and didn't like to get my face wet, so I pretended to swim, waving my arms in the water while firmly keeping my feet on the bottom.

"Look, I'm swimming" I would call out.

Our teachers knew quite well what I was doing but responded with "Well done," and "Keep going."

Eventually, I learned the wonderful buoyancy of the blue-green water and let it hold me up while I practiced the dog paddle, the Deadman's Float, and the Crawl. Then there was no stopping me. I was not a sports swimmer, but I enjoyed the baths, and graduated to the larger pool in a few summers. Here I became very bold and took to jumping off the top diving board, which seemed very high to us back then. I was not too keen on the deeper water at the diving end and always kept a look out for "sharks". After our swim there would be crisps and hot chocolate from the vending machine in the foyer and the glow that comes from youthful exercise.

## MR. GRIMES THE SHOE SHOP

Because of Bristol's close relationship with Wales, across the Severn Channel, many trades-people were known both by their family name and the name of their trade. Welsh tradition gave folks two names, like "Mr. Jones the Butcher". I think that this was because there were so many Welsh Jones, Evans, and Powells, that this practice sorted them all out and people knew who-was-who.

We knew Mr. Grimes the Shoe Shop when we were growing up. A small, dapper Welshman, Mr. Grimes owned a small shop up in Bristol, close to St. Paul's. He not only managed the shop but came to the house, once a week, to collect payments for the shoes that Mum bought on credit. He came so frequently and punctually that, when I was little, I thought he was a relative! Most of our shoes came as hand-me downs from relatives and neighbors. Children often outgrow their shoes before they outwear them. However, every spring Mum would take Alan and me up to Mr. Grimes shop to buy new Clark's leather sandals. These would be identical ones for both Alan and me, because, being kinder to my shoes, I could pass mine onto Alan who often outwore his shoes at an alarming rate. We usually bought reddish, leather sandals for school and I got white sandals for Sunday School and special occasions.

Our feet were squeezed and measured with a long, sliding ruler and we were always cautioned to wear clean, ankle socks for the occasion. In the fifties, Mr. Grimes purchased a machine that x-rayed your feet inside your new shoes, to see if they fit. It was quite fun to put on new shoes and to look down the small porthole to see the bones of your feet surrounded by shoe nails. Later, these machines were considered dangerous, both to the customers and the shop assistant, and were removed. I often wonder if Mr. Grime's death from cancer was as a result of using this machine.

We got sandals for the summer, lace-ups for the winter and, later, little-heeled shoes for me as I became a teenager. Mum and Dad got footwear there, too, and it was a point of pride in the family to have well-cared-for shoes. Dad's Army training came out as he insisted on us all polishing our footwear once a week with Kiwi shoe polish. This was not a favorite activity for Alan and me. Dad would extort us to "Put some elbow grease into it!" to get us moving along with the chore. The shoes did look nice when they were done though. Later, in my twenties, I learned a trick from a hiking school, about putting shoe polish onto wet leather to preserve them. It seemed to do the trick.

It is interesting how shoes define the generations. Children today mostly wear trainers or sneakers. They no longer wear gym shoes (we called them Plimsols) or lace-ups. No longer do they shine their shoes or take a pride in their footwear except in relation to how much they cost. But then I remember my mother telling me about the wooden clogs that she had to wear to school, and the boots with many buttons that had to be fastened with a "boot latch", that they wore in the winter. Grampy Tanzell was forever repairing their shoes and boots himself because they cost so much. Perhaps children are happier and more carefree with their modern footwear.

## GORAM'S FAIR

There is a local Bristol legend about two giants, Goram and Vincent, who fell in love with the same woman. Her name was Avona and she was described as a "Wiltshire-born merry belle". She made a promise that she would marry the first of the giants who could drain a great lake that stretched from Bradford-on-Avon to Bristol. The giants, Goram and Vincent picked different routes to drain this great body of water. Goram decided to work through the Henbury Hills and Vincent chose Durdham Downs. The brothers were quite different. Goram got thirsty and in the heat of the day, drank a quantity of beer and fell asleep in a large armchair. Vincent, who was more industrious, kept digging until he drained the lake at nearby Sea Mills. Vincent was the winner and Avona gave herself to him. She also gave her name to the Gorge that Vincent had formed with his digging: the Avon Gorge.

Goram awoke and was broken-hearted that he had not won the contest or Avona's heart. He was said to have hurled himself into the Severn where he drowned. Two flattish islands, which stick up out of the Severn Estuary, are named Flat Holm and Steep Holm. They are claimed to be Goram's head and shoulder emerging up out of the Severn mud. Vincent's name was also honored when some steep rocks were named after him, close to where the Clifton Suspension Bridge now crosses the Avon Gorge. Goram's seat, a chair-shaped rock can also be seen in the vicinity. There's even another version of the tale that had Goram building the Avon Gorge by himself, but he died after tripping on a "tump" of land known as Maes Knoll, an Iron Age hill fort at neighboring Dundry Hill.

Every summer a great fair was held at Blaise Castle estate, close to Blaise Castle House. The Castle is not really a castle but a folly that was built in the grounds of the big house. The House was eventually turned into a wonderful museum that housed dolls, historical clothing and farm implements, dolls houses, and models of country life from earlier centuries. In the cellars were dioramas of local craftsmen: a barrel cooper, a top hat maker, and other ancient trades. Out front there was a lawn and a shallow wading pool that was much enjoyed by the Shire children in the summer.

Here, every year, was erected a large talking model of Goram. Judging by photos from that era, Goram's seated model must have been about thirty feet high. His shiny black boots were as tall as an average man and his head about the same size. Several times a day, a recorded voice told the story of Goram and Vincent while sports events and games took place in Blaise Castle grounds. Further up, in the big field, a funfair was set up that lasted well into the night. There were stalls where prizes could be won for throwing a hoop over a bottle, fishing a small duck out of water, or throwing a coin onto lucky numbers. We didn't believe the giant's story for a minute, but it was all great fun.

## THE SWEET SHOPS

An important part of our childhood lives were the sweetshops of Shire. There were several of these and each one had its own character. The closest to Meadow Grove was Baldocks. On entering the shop, the sweet counter was to your left and the paper shop to your right. The paper shop also sold Golden Virginia tobacco, cigarette papers and cigarettes. Many times, Mum would send me down to Baldocks for "Five Woodbines", cheap cigarettes, which I would take home in a white, paper bag.

On pocket-money days, we would troop down to the sweet shop and spend a considerable amount of time surveying the sweets and deciding on our purchases. We were urged to "Hurry up, decide what you want!" There would be round, flying-saucer shaped wafers filled with fizzy powder, "sherbert" fountains: tubes filled with the same fizzy powder, penny and "ha'penny" chews, four-for-a penny Black Jacks, more colored, fizzy powder that would be made into a kind of lemonade, packets of Jelly Babies and Chocolate Buttons, tubes of Smarties, Polo Mints, and Rowntree's Fruit Gums, bars of Nestle's chocolate, and loads of black licorice: ropes, twirls, shapes, and All Sorts. In great glass jars were sweets that were weighed out in 2oz portions and slid into little, white, paper bags: Satins, Lemon Drops, Sour Pear Drops, Peanut Clusters, Mint Imperials, and Nut Toffees.

Once a week Dad would send us down to Baldocks to pay for the week's Evening Post newspapers and to pick up our magazines and comics. Mum always got Women's Own, and Dad read The Norton: all about motorbikes. Alan and I shared the Dandy, the Beano, the Topper, the Eagle, Girl, Bunty, or the Beazer, whatever our friends were reading dictated our choice. Quite often we caught Dad reading our comics!

There were other sweet shops, too. The Clark brothers ran two shops, one up in the village and the other, newer one, closer to Avonmouth. In between was a small sweet shop opposite the Estate Office in Shire, but both buildings got demolished in the later 1950s. Lots of other shops sold sweets but we were mostly faithful to Baldocks and the Clarks.

Of course, all these sweets soon necessitated a dreaded trip to the dentist. This meant visiting the office of Dr. Dawes the Dentist. His waiting room was like a museum filled with wonderful souvenirs from his travels: turtle shells, drums, and stuffed animals. This took our mind somewhat off the visit upstairs, but we still feared the walk up the staircase to Mr. Dawes surgery. Being post-war Britain, we had the luxury of gas to ease the pain of the fillings and extractions, but it was still a scary process. However, it didn't put us off our sweets and we would be back the next day at the sweet shop.

## STREET GAMES

Meadow Grove did not get a lot of traffic, particularly during the day time. Kids had all the back gardens and the street in which to play. And play we did! There were small group games such as Mothers and Fathers where we sent my brother Alan and the other boys "off to work" so we girls could have the garden and our dolls to ourselves. Alan would retaliate by threatening to eat Spot's dog biscuits, and when we dared him, he did! We tied skipping ropes to gates and jumped Higher and Higher, skipped to rhymes such as

*Down in the valley where the green grass grows,*
*Dear little Angela she grows like a rose,*
*She grows, she grows, she grows, so sweet,*
*That she calls for her boyfriend down the street*

and many other rhymes that had been passed down from older child to younger child. We rolled colorful, glass marbles in the gutters and bounced balls off walls and roofs. We chalked Hopscotch diagrams in the street and rolled stones before hopping through the sequences. We played group games, running from side to side across the street playing games such as Please Mr. Wolf Can We Cross the Water, Chain Touch, and Colored Eggs. In the summer we were out playing right after school, only going home for supper, then right out again to play until the sun set and there was no more light, when we were called home to bed.

In the back gardens we played Dress Up with clothing we scrounged from church jumble sales and ancient aunties, we put on amateur plays, we cooperated in games of Hide and Seek, Touch, and Statues. We formed strong, social bonds with neighborhood kids and fought feuds with children from the surrounding street with rotten apples and stones. I don't remember any kids getting seriously hurt but our fighting fury was certainly strong, perhaps even tribal. There were trees and sheds to climb, bikes and roller skates to share, and when exhausted we would sit down and talk, and talk, and talk about everything under the sun. I am not sure now what we talked about, but we seemed to put the world to rights. We were children of invention: pre-TV, post-war, creative, and forever busy with our imaginations.

## THE BROWNIES

Like most little girls in post-war England I wanted to join the Brownies, the younger version of the Girl Guides. I had to wait a whole year to join but I practiced the salute and the pledge with girls in the street who were older than me. They seemed so grown up with their neat, brown dresses, and folded neckerchiefs that could be used as a sling in an emergency. Each week they proudly showed me the badges they had earned, and their proud mums would sew the patches onto their uniforms. I so wanted to be like them, to wear the uniform and to earn the colorful badges.

Soon, my birthday came along, and I badgered Mum, every day, to join the Brownie troop up in Shire. Mum was able to get a secondhand uniform from another family, whose daughter had tried the Brownies and got tired of it. We had to take all the patches off and wash and press the uniform, but it looked "good as new". I practiced and practiced, folding the kerchief until I had it just right. I already had the Brownie Handbook and knew how many fingers wide to make the kerchief and how to slide it into the little, leather ring. I looked forward to getting lots of badges.

How I loved the Brownies. Unfortunately, it didn't last long! My initial enthusiasm went the way of all youthful enthusiasm, but I loved the time that I was in the troop. We learned to identify leaves and insects, played games where we would creep stealthily up on each other, held elfin rituals with woodland names, around a make-belief toadstool, had wonderful parties and learned lots of useful skills, like how to make a good cup of tea! I didn't earn too many badges, but I had a lot of fun. It was one more step on the road to growing up and becoming part of the Shire community.

## THE WIRELESS

The lilting theme tune of The Archers takes me back in time to my childhood home. Immediately I am back in our living room, listening to the wireless, as we expectantly devoured the latest events happening to the folk in the country village of Ambridge. The Archers relayed the "gentle lives of country folk" daily. We were as familiar with the radio characters as our own family members. We struggled with the farmer as he delivered a reluctant calf, cried as local people died and others were born, and celebrated birthdays, anniversaries, and weddings with them. The Archers became part of our extended family.

This was not because we didn't already have family. Our Grandparents, aunts and uncles and numerous cousins, many times removed, all lived in the same town, mostly in the village. But the Archers gave us a daily run-down of events that we didn't even follow in our own families. We were confidant to every Ambridge secret that was whispered to a friend, we worried when Dad Archer was in the hospital, and felt outrage when an injustice took place. We became socialized to a greater world outside of our village, town and city. This was an era when things were simpler, relationships were less complex, and we became part of a larger world outside of our insular lives.

Before we started attending school, another radio favorite was Listen with Mother. Mum would turn on the radio and sit us in the large armchair by the fire. First came a short piece of classical music: Berceuse from Faure's Dolly Suite, followed by nursery rhymes and a short story. The program started at a quarter to two and lasted fifteen minutes, time enough for Mum to do the dinner dishes and have a quick cigarette. After the music would come chimes, "Ding-de-dong, Ding-de-dong, Ding, Ding" and the voice of Catherine Edwards asked "Are you sitting comfortably? Then I'll begin." Nursery rhymes followed: *Ride a Cock Horse to Banbury Cross, Rub-a-Dub-Dub, Three Men in a Tub*, and *Mary, Mary, Quite Contrary, How Does Your Garden Grow*. My favorite was *I Love Little Kitten, her Coat is so Warm*, as our black cat, Tiny, often curled up with us to listen. Next was a short story, intended for little children, such as "Mitten the Kitten." Another radio program, that delighted us as children, was Toy Town with stuttering Larry the Lamb and practical Dennis the Dachshund.

Our next-door neighbors, Mr. and Mrs. Heal, bought a black and white television set in the 1950s and this was a great novelty to the neighborhood. Aunty Marge and Uncle Arthur, up on Springfield Avenue, also had a tiny set but all they seemed to watch was horse racing and football. Mrs. Heal would call Alan and me, over the hedge, to come round and watch TV in the afternoons. We looked forward to the black and white runs of Andy Pandy (with Looby Loo and Teddy), and Bill and Ben, the Flowerpot Men programs. Their co-star, Weed, had very few lines that consisted mainly of her saying "Weeeeeeed!" Alan and I started talking like Bill and Ben, "Flobbadobbadobdob," until Mum made us stop. We couldn't afford television so going to the Heals was a great treat. We were relatively well-behaved when we visited next door. We quietly sat through the shows until Andy and Teddy would sing "Time to go home, time to go home, Andy is waving goodbye!" and we would happily run off home.

## SPRING DOWN BARRACKS LANE

Spring seemed to come suddenly around the beginning of April. The March winds could be fierce, but the bitter cold of winter was becoming just a memory. We called the spring winds "lazy winds" because they went right through you instead of going around! Just before Easter, signs of spring would begin to show around the village. The fruit trees would show a hint of blossom and gardens would sprout with snowdrops, crocuses, and daffodils.

Near our house on Meadow Grove was an old road called Barracks Lane. During the two World Wars soldiers had pitched their tents here and housed their horses, before being shipped off to foreign parts. It probably had some other, ancient, name before but this had been lost over time.

Here were fields, hedgerows, cows, horses, and a couple of farms. However, the further you walked down Barracks Lane, the blacker everything became. The end of the Lane reached as far as Avonmouth Industrial Estate: the carbon black factory, fertilizer plant, and smelting works.

Before the era of environmental safety, these firms belched out pollutants that contaminated everything around them. The trees, the grass, even the wool on the sheep in the nearby fields, were covered in black dust. But through this backdrop of darkness came spring! Tiny green leaves pushed through the grime, hazel catkins and pussy willow buds showed pale green and silver, and golden celandines shone in the hedgerows. A promise that even though humans could contaminate their surroundings, nature would heal with new growth every new spring.

As the weather warmed up, we would go looking for tadpoles down the Rhine. This lazy stream of water leached off the saltmarshes below Kingsweston. It ended up draining into a barred drain to make its way to the River Avon. At its deepest it was probably only a couple of feet, but we were always wary of its murky depths. Here we caught crested newts, sticklebacks, and tadpoles. There was always loads of clumped frog spawn, looking like black-dotted tapioca pudding, and strings of long toad spawn. We would take the spawn home in a jam-jar and watch the tadpoles develop from vegetarian pond-scum eaters to voracious carnivores that would devour each other if we didn't provide fish food. As the tiny froglets developed their legs and lost their tails, we would troop down to the Rhine, to let them go back into the stream. We didn't need lessons in nature: we lived through it every season in Shire.

# EASTER

Easter, of course meant Easter Eggs but there was more to Easter weekend that just the chocolate. On Good Friday Dad would pick up a bag full of Hot Cross Buns from the bakery. These yeasty, sweet, bread rolls had an X incised into the top and were glazed with a sugary covering. These were to remind us of the death of Jesus on the cross. I think they also had a pagan significance from our Celtic past. We didn't go to church on Good Friday, but we usually had it off from school. The buns were eaten without butter or jam as they were sweet enough and often had currants in them. Our house was usually decorated with early spring blooms, particularly lambs-tail catkins and pussy willows with their little, silvery buds. There were daffodils, too, if it hadn't been too hard a winter although I have seen daffodils pushing their way up through the snow. Other spring flowers that defied the cold and frost were snowdrops, aptly named, as clusters of them routinely burst into blossom before the snows had fully melted. Their bright, green leaves and deceptively fragile, white blossoms were a welcome sign of spring.

Saturday usually meant relatives: grandparents, aunts and uncles visiting our house and with hushed whispers handing Mum rustling, paper bags that were secreted somewhere in the house. Mum, too, coming home from the shops with the groceries, hurried packages upstairs. As we got older, we learned where the hiding places were. The bags were never in the airing cupboard as this was too warm. They were often in the back of Mum and Dad's wardrobe in their unheated bedroom. We usually sneaked a peek to see what sort of eggs we would get on Sunday morning. If we were good on Saturday, Mum would let us have a few, small, Cadbury's eggs as a treat. But the bounty came on Sunday morning.

Easter morning the bells from St. Mary's Parish Church, up in the village, would wake us, tolling the good news of the Resurrection. Mum would cook us a fry-up for breakfast: eggs, bacon, sausage, tomatoes, and fried bread, to try and fill us up before the great chocolate experience!

The inevitable happened and we got our eggs. Some were small, hollow, chocolate eggs wrapped in silver foil in fancy-shaped eggcups, which Mum retrieved to be used for our morning breakfast eggs. Usually these egg cups were in the form of rabbits, chickens, or other Easter symbols. Next came the big eggs! These were splendid affairs: gift boxed, wrapped in colored foil, two chocolate shells to each egg, filled with Smarties, Maltesers, or Quality Street chocolates. We would get four or five each. Mum always admonished us to "save some for later." Of course, we didn't eat all the eggs at once and Mum wisely saved some for us.

Easter mid-day dinner was always a leg of lamb with mint sauce, new potatoes, garden peas (which I helped to pick and shell), and gravy. However, much chocolate we had eaten we always ate Easter dinner.

After dinner we would wash, change into our best clothes, and walk up the village to Sunday School. Here, in a flower-filled church we lustily sang time-honored hymns to celebrate the rebirth: *Christ the Lord is Risen Today*, *All Things Bright and Beautiful*, and *Thine is the Glory*. As we sang, sweet, chocolate memories filled our minds and souls. Easter was a beautiful time for children of all ages!

## THE BALLET SCHOOL

One spring, when I was about eight years old, I told Mum that I wanted to go to the ballet school up off Springfield Avenue. Some of my school friends at Avon Primary went there. Their descriptions of the multicolored outfits, recitals and pointy shoes caught my imagination. As a child I was always twirling and skipping but here was a chance to really dance!

Mum bought me pink ballet slippers at the shoe shop, but we had to take them back because they were toe- shoes, with a blocked point. I was not quite ready for those! With my new, soft, ballet slippers and wearing the little, white practice outfit that Mum sewed on her old Singer, I was ready to dance.

At the first class, everybody at the school seemed more knowledgeable than me. But they showed me where to change and how to lace up my shoes. Soon, I became adept at the foot positions at the bar. However, I wasn't so good at remembering directions. Perhaps because of my myopia, or the fact that my left handedness had been switched at school, I had a hard time with lefts and rights, and sequential directions. When everybody else would turn to the right, I would find myself facing left. The ballet mistress was very patient, and I learned to love the accompanying, tinkling piano and ballet routines. I soared home after the first class in a cloud of euphoria.

The joy did not last though as we were relatively poor, and Mum could not afford the weekly fees or the expensive recital outfits that Mums were expected to sew. I missed the first recital even though I continued to practice right up to the day of the performance. Somehow the joy had gone out of the dance and I decided to stop. It was one of those unfilled dreams that never seem to become actualized. I had chances as an adult to take classes, but I never fully recaptured the joy of those early ballet lessons.

## THE COOPERATIVE STORE

Situated next to St. Mary's Parish Church were the three Cooperative shops: a general food store, a butcher's shop, and a general store where you could buy anything from a little, tin tray to shoes. The old Coop (pronounced co-op) buildings were torn down in the 1970s to be replaced by a generic supermarket that was still called the Coop but lacked the old-time atmosphere.

The Cooperative movement was started by the Socialists and centered round the concept of joint ownership. When Shire villagers shopped at the Cooperative stores, they earned dividends: cash amounts that could be traded for food, clothing, and household items. Mum was proud of her "divi" book that recorded the amounts that she had saved by shopping at the Coop. This manner of shopping did take away trade from some of the smaller village shops, but most families also shopped "up the village" to supplement what they couldn't get at the Coop. We shopped at the Coop because Nana Win was a staunch Labor supporter and the Coop was part of their plan for society.

The Coop food store boasted a new-fangled device called a deep freeze. This was about the size of a modern fridge lying on its back with an open top. Frozen fish and ice cream could be purchased from the freezer, but Mum preferred to buy fresh fish up the village, from the fish monger. Shopping carts had not yet been introduced, so women, who did most of the shopping, still brought their own cloth bags and wicker baskets to the shops. Some weekly shopping of staples was done but, mostly, women would shop daily.

Next door was the Coop butcher shop, its windows hung with sausages, plucked chickens, geese, and ducks. On tiled slabs in the window were joints of beef, pork chops, and legs of lamb, liver, tripe, and other offal foods, that nobody would eat today. Behind the clean and gleaming glass counter inside worked two burly, red-faced butchers. They chopped and sliced the meat on an ancient wooden block of wood and stored whole sides of cows and pigs in a walk-in freezer. The butchers were known to have favorites among the housewives and would throw in a "bit extra" if they liked the lady or if she was a relative.

The third shop ran the length of the way from the High Street to Pembroke Road and was a veritable emporium of goods. Housewives could be seen browsing the store, putting items aside, until they could save enough, or putting money into a Christmas account so that they could buy gifts and food for the holidays. Here could be found oilcloth for the kitchen table, linens, and many other household items.

At the back of the Coop on Pembroke Road was a display window for the household store and an anonymous-looking door that led up some narrow stairs to the meeting hall above. Here met various philanthropic orders, political and religious groups. There was a stage and a piano, a large hall with a scrubbed, wooden-floor, and a small kitchen at the rear. Once a week, children would meet here for a social club where we sang in a choir, painted pottery, wove baskets and played games. It was a lot of fun and Alan and I attended for several years, eventually becoming helpers. The Coop not only provided our food and furniture but also our social activities.

## SUNDAY SCHOOL

Alan and I were taken to Sunday School beginning at two years of age. Shirehampton Baptist Church was our first, spiritual home and we gained the greater part of our religious education there. Baptists only believed in adult baptism, so held a service of Dedication for infants. Babies' names were then written on a large Cradle Roll poster that was hung in the Sunday School.

During the immediate postwar years, the Baptist Sunday School took place at historic Kingsweston House while renovations were completed. After the war, the Baby Boom took place and churches had to expand their premises to accommodate all the children. The Baptist Sunday School was no exception. Older children met in the church, but younger children gathered each Sunday in the wooden hut at the back of the church. Here a pot-bellied stove provided heat in the winter and rows of chairs were regularly filled with washed, combed and neat children from the Shire neighborhood.

The youngest children sat in tiny chairs at the back and were ushered out, part of the way through the service, to play in the church vestry, where there was a large sand tray. They couldn't be expected to sit still through all the hymns and lessons. We older children sang seasonal hymns accompanied by the piano: *Jesus Wants Me for a Sunbeam*, *Praise Him, Praise Him, All Ye little Children*, and *All Things Bright and Beautiful*. We would then break into classes for Bible instruction. The teachers tried to make Sunday School fun with religious stickers that we could collect, special services like Mothering Sunday, but it was still Sunday School.

As Alan and I got older we graduated to the Church for Sunday School. Here large, wooden, wall panels could be swung out to make classrooms and we earned children's books for good attendance. Several times a year the children would give a Presentation and we learned parts which represented Bible stories.

One year, I had to learn a poem about the Great Flood, but I caught German Measles and had to quickly teach it to Alan, who took my place. Decades later we both could still remember the verse:

> *How lovely is the rainbow arch, red, orange, yellow, green;*
> *Blue, indigo and violet, upon the dark cloud seen;*
> *A token of God's covenant that he will not destroy*
> *This Earth again with watery flood;*
> *The sight fills us with joy!*

By the time that I was twelve and Alan nine, the Baptist Sunday School failed to keep us interested. We drifted away to eventually join the new Pentecostal Church up near the Clay Quarry. Mum and Dad were upset but let us decide where we wanted to worship. They were not strong church goers. I imagine they thought "Better any church, than no church!" It didn't do us any harm and perhaps did us some good in the long run.

# PRIMARY SCHOOL

First school days (back row, far left)

Avon Primary was a very special school. It was built post-WWII and was intended to give children a comprehensive education, not just the three Rs: reading, writing and arithmetic. My first years of primary schooling took place at Shirehampton Infants School and I have memories of smelly, outside toilets, a scary head teacher, and of feeling quite lost. The move to Avon Primary was exciting. Here was a modern school, with big, sunny classrooms, lots of space for adventure, exploration and learning. Children were considered intelligent creatures that just needed the right environment to grow and learn. It was very much an experimental school and our headteacher, Mrs. Wendy Haywood, brought in music, color, activity, creativity, literature, and art. Prints by famous artists lined the walls, we listened to exciting musical works, replicated them with percussion instruments, and we wrote and directed our own plays. Reading was encouraged and we were read to with regularity. Mid-lesson we would be told to put down our pencils and Mr. Cox or Mr. Parker would read to us. They read Mill on the Floss, Wind in the Willows, and the Lion, the Witch, and the Wardrobe that excited our imaginations. The students were entered into poetry and art competitions. It turned out that I was good at writing poetry and once that tap got turned on it didn't stop. We learned about civic responsibilities by creating a wall map of an imaginary village and tackled problems, as if they were real ones, by using our writing, and arithmetic skills.

While the focus was on creativity, the fundamentals were not forgotten, and mathematics was a major focus of every day. Unfortunately, I was not good at multiplication and at remembering the times-table. I envied the kids who could reel off the seven and nine times-tables by heart. I was a daydreamer and often got lost in my own imagination when I should have been memorizing a poem or multiplication.

Outside of our classroom windows were wonderful, flower gardens with roses and large trees. On bright days the classrooms were flooded with sunshine and the natural light made a big difference to our school work and attention. School photos show us bright-eyed, eager and cheerful, different from the school photos of my mother's era when the children appeared malnourished and dull-eyed by comparison. We were the promised generation, the children born from the rubble of a Second World War, the Baby Boom, and the pledge that things would be better for this new generation of Bristolians.

# THE GHOST OF MEADOW GROVE

Meadow Grove

Our house, 40 Meadow Grove had a ghost. It was not a destructive ghost, just noisy and playful: a poltergeist. When Alan and I were upstairs we would hear footsteps on the thinly-carpeted stairs. My bedroom faced the landing, which was lit from a street light outside. Although the footsteps came to the top of the stairs nothing came into sight. We called our parents, but they didn't believe us.

At other times, there would be noises in our parents' bedroom although nobody was in there. The springs on the bed could be heard, as if someone was bouncing, and the wardrobe door would spring open, with a bang, as it hit the wall. Nobody believed us so we stopped telling people about the ghost.

However, when we were grown, my Mum, Alan's young daughter, Joy, and I visited the street and stopped outside the house. A man came out and introduced himself as the house's current tenant. I tentatively asked him about the ghost. Very animated, he related how his family had encountered the ghost when they moved in. His children talked about faces on the ceiling and footsteps on the stairs. One day, his wife came home to see an apparition of an older woman with her arm on the fire mantelshelf. What was interesting was that her elbow was higher up, where the old mantle had been before renovations. The apparition had a tea towel over her arm, and she was staring into the corner by the fireplace.

The current tenant made some inquiries, to find that the original residents of the house were a mother and son. Apparently, the son suffered from depression and the mother took care of him. The son committed suicide and the mother was bereft. It seemed as if she was still looking out for her son. The tenant asked the local Catholic priest to come in and bless the house.

Distant relatives are now tenants in the house, and they report that the disturbances are still happening, particularly on the staircase.

## THE UNICORN HORN

All the children in our neighborhood had dens. There were dens constructed of branches and leaves up in Penpole Woods, dens behind garden sheds, and dens in cupboards. Anywhere there was a space where several children could hide and store a few comics, a bottle of Tizer pop, apples and sweets became a potential den. I suppose that the idea of dens came from our adventure comic books or the Saturday morning films at the Savoy Cinema.

Alan and I had a series of dens. One, during the summer, was in our coal bunker. Mum found it and was cross because we had used her good pillows. The cupboard under the stairs was a great place for a den and we had a permanent one there, for many years, stocked with comics, old quilts, and pillows. We had candles, too, until Mum banned them and bought us battery torches. The cupboard under the stairs filled my dreams with wonderful possibilities. In one dream, I discovered a sliver of light that came from a secret door that led to a magical world of talking fishes and magic boxes.

We shared dens up at Penpole Woods with our friends, making forays to collect Spanish chestnuts, blackberries, and hazelnuts for our "larders". We would have raiding parties where we would leap out at unsuspecting walkers in the woods, especially if they had children and dogs with them. If another group took over our dens, there was outright war with stones and branches being thrown. We became little savages, perhaps displaying our tribal, Celtic roots, as we rousted the offending kids from our woodland territory.

Another of our dens was behind the shed in our back garden. A couple of rain-hardened cement bags made seats and tarps became a roof. While constructing this den we made a wonderful discovery. We found a unicorn horn under the hedge! We were so excited! We decided to keep it a secret as this was a treasure beyond anything we could imagine. We hid the unicorn horn under layers of comics and leaves.

Eventually we could hold in the excitement no more and told Angela, who lived next door, and Gillian, who lived a few houses down. They were sworn to secrecy. However, they eventually told their parents who talked to our Mum and Dad, who demanded to see the unicorn horn. At first, they were as puzzled and amazed as us but, after a few discreet inquiries, the horn was identified as coming from a narwhale.

Narwhales are toothed whales belonging to the same family as sperm and pilot whales, dolphins and porpoises. Their scientific name *Monodon Monoceros* means "the one toothed animal that looks like a unicorn." The narwhale lives only in arctic seas so the horn may have been brought back to the port of Bristol by a sailor. Narwhale horns grow to over eight feet but ours was only a few feet long. So, it probably belonged to a young narwhale or it may have been a secondary horn that narwhales sometimes grow.

We were disappointed and still clung to some faint hope that this was indeed a unicorn horn that had been misidentified. The horn was eventually taken to school where it was put on display in the corridor leading to the Infants. Other kids saw it, identified as a narwhale horn, but we kept the myth going that it was really a unicorn horn that we had found behind our garden shed.

# THE QUEEN'S CORONATION

Queen's Coronation Party, Meadow Grove

The second Tuesday of June 1953 was a little stormy and showers came in later that day. For the previous two weeks Mum had been making costumes for Alan and me to wear at the celebration of Queen Elizabeth II's Coronation. Alan would be a pixie in a green outfit with bells sewn on his shoes and pointed hat. I was to be a fairy with silver wings made from tinfoil. It was an exciting time as we watched festival bunting being raised above the street and listened in on plans to hold a party for the children at the Meadow Grove Housing Office.

The day of the Coronation started off with street games. A rope was stretched across the road and buns were tied with string at intervals. This game was mainly for the adults as they competed to eat a bun as quickly as possible without using their hands. There were races too: Egg and Spoon, Three-Legged Race, and a Sack Race.

They must have closed off the street to traffic for the day because no cars came by to interrupt the street games. After the games, we all paraded down to the Housing Office and our costumes were judged: I think it was one of our school friends Gillian or Jean, who won with a beautiful crinoline costume representing Bo Peep. One of the Lloyd boys came as a chimney sweep with his dad's brushes. We rushed home, to change into our party clothes, and back to the Housing Office.

The back room of the Housing Office was decorated with red, white and blue garlands and tables arranged in long rows with every type of party food imaginable. First, I believe, we listened to a radio broadcast of the Coronation and gifts were given out: blue, glass, souvenir beakers; bone china mugs; and little mirrors, all with the Queens portrait.

The party seemed to go on for a long time and the food kept coming. Eventually, we were all called out to the little grassy hill opposite the Housing Office for a group picture. Alan got sent home with Dad, as they both got tired and grumpy, but Mum and I joined the group as snapshots were taken. I have this photo, with Mum and me still wearing our party hats, trying to shield ourselves from the coming rainstorm. There had been beer for some of the adults and one neighbor came out with a large tea kettle and squatted in the front row. A good cup of tea was what we needed after all the excitement and we were happy to troop home for a good "cuppa" tea.

# THE LITTLE THEATRE

About once a month, Nana Win would take me with her and her lady friends to the Bristol Little Theatre. Situated about eight miles from Shire, in the Bristol City Centre, the Little Theatre was a very special treat. In the morning of the trip, Nana would let me pick bunches of diminutive flowers from her summer garden: mauve violets, pink clarkia, multi-colored sweet-scented stock, white alyssum and yellow, baby rosebuds. Grampy Jim would save me foil paper from his cigarette packets and I would peel off the tobacco-scented tissue from the foil. These would make little silver squares, just right for wrapping small posies of flowers for Nana and her friends.

The posies would take me most of the morning to assemble and I had them ready for Nana's friends by lunchtime. Nana would provide safety pins and, as the ladies arrived, they would pin one of my posies to their ample bosoms. The ladies: Mrs. Daniels, Mrs. Coombs, Mrs. Bull and other lady neighbors would turn up in their pretty dresses, with freshly set hair, smelling of Eau-de-Cologne. Nana would have already washed, dried and combed my curly hair and made sure that I was wearing a clean dress, white ankle socks, and freshly-whitened sandals. Nana had crocheted the lacey socks herself from mercerized cotton. If the weather was cool, I would wear a small, hand-knit sweater. My favorite was a white angora bolero, which Mum had made for me for Aunty Mary's wedding. When everybody was ready, Grampy Jim would head off to dig in his garden, and we ladies would take off for the Theatre. It wasn't far to walk up to catch the number 28 bus on Shirehampton Green and ride into Bristol. We were full of anticipation.

The Little Theatre was in the space above the entrance foyer to the Colston Hall which itself had an ancient heritage. In the 13th Century the site housed a Carmelite friary and by Tudor times a Great House graced the site. Queen Elizabeth 1st was said to have stayed there in 1574. In 1707 the site became Colston Boys School but by 1867 it had been rebuilt with a wonderful brick and tile, vaulted façade by Foster and Wood. The Little Theatre hosted both the Bristol Repertory Company and the Rapier Players. It was the fourth theatre to grace the site, having suffered two major fires and two World Wars.

The Theatre was a delight and I would sit rapt with wonder as the actors played out their stories. The excitement was not over, as Nana, the ladies and I made our way to the restaurant where afternoon tea would be waiting for us. Tea time consisted of pots of freshly brewed tea, milk and sugar, and cream cakes. As the youngest, I was always allowed to have first choice of the cakes! I felt very special, as my brother Alan, was considered too young and too distractible to come to the Theatre.

# BRISTOL ZOO

Alan, Dad and Angela at the Zoo

Several times a year, Mum and Dad would take us up to visit Bristol Zoo. The Zoo was situated near the center of Bristol, up on the Downs. The Downs was a high, flat, grassy area, of several square miles, that were used in ancient times as grazing land. One side of the Downs plunged down to the Avon Gorge where the River Avon flowed into Bristol Docks. Isambard Kingdom Brunel's famous iron suspension bridge could be crossed here into Leigh Woods from the Downs. Another side of the Zoo faced the Downs and the remainder bordered onto Edwardian residences, where the roars of the lions and tigers greeted sunrise and sunset.

A high, whitewashed wall surrounded the small Victorian Zoo and images of the animals were stenciled in black on the white stucco. Mum packed jam sandwiches, Cornish pasties, and a flask of hot, sweet tea for a picnic and we always took our coats in case it rained or turned cold, which it often did. We took the double-decker bus up to the Zoo and we could hardly sit in our seats as we were so excited.

On the bus we planned our day. "Well, first, we'll do the cages with the lions and tigers, and orangutans." And of course, we had to visit Alfred! Alfred was a huge, venerable, wise-looking (and probably wise-thinking) lowland gorilla who had a cage all to himself. Everybody loved Alfred and came to talk to him and express pity that he was locked up by himself. Personally, I think he liked the privacy as the younger apes in the adjoining cage were always throwing things at each other. Such was the love for Alfred that, when he died, he was stuffed and put in the Bristol Museum.

All the cages had an outside area and an indoor part. On cold days many of the animals would be indoors, swaying listlessly and bored, and as interested in us, as we were in them. We always had a planned route around the zoo: the big cats and the apes, the snake pit, the aquarium, the smaller monkeys, (stop for an ice-cream), the sea lion pond at feeding time, the giraffes and okapis, the polar bear and brown bear pits, (stop for a picnic on the lawn), the monkey temple, buy peanuts for the capuchins and, (of course, some for us), the kangaroos and the wallabies, the ducks on the lake, and the parrots swinging out on portable perches in the huge fir trees, the penguin habitat, and the flamingos, until we came to Rosie.

Rosie was a very old, Indian elephant, who had been at the zoo since Mum and Dad were little. She carried children, in a howdah on her back, once around the park. We paid a penny for a ride and she took the big, copper pennies from our outstretched hands and put them in the keeper's pocket. She would kneel and we would climb the short, wooden steps up to the howdah, where we were fastened in and we would begin our lumbering, perambulation around the park. After Rosie, we would try and do the route again, but, by this time, Mum and Dad would be getting tired and grumpy, and we would decide to make our way home. We never wanted to leave. "Just one more visit to say goodnight to Alfred!"

In later years, the Zoo became more progressive, and friendly animals were paired up: kangaroos with emus, and young gorillas with chimps. One year my parents exclaimed "Look at the little animals they've put in the elephant enclosure! What are they?" Upon further inspection, the "little animals" turned out to be elephant dung. We didn't let Mum and Dad forget that! The Zoo was a magical place, educational, entertaining, and never to be forgotten.

## HARVEST FESTIVAL

Americans may have their Thanksgiving, but we had our Harvest Festival. The sounds and smells of Harvest Festival will stay with me forever. Each time I smell the scent of apples it takes me back to Shirehampton Baptist Church sanctuary at this special time of year. Around the middle of September, we would receive notes from Sunday School to start bringing in tins of food. Mum complained, as it was hard enough for her to feed us all on Dad's Smelting Works wages, so we usually ended up taking in bags of apples, flowers and vegetables from our garden. This was usual for families that didn't have much but we were thankful for what we did have.

In the weeks leading up to Harvest Festival the children of the village would comb the hedgerows, picking sprays of berries: hawthorn and rose hips, and yew. We pulled ivy off tree trunks and trailers of honeysuckle gone to seed, that we called Old Man's Beard. Michaelmas Daisies from local gardens added a touch of blue to the festive theme. Holly trees in the neighborhood were pruned to provide sprigs of green with shiny red berries but I don't ever remember mistletoe being brought into the church. Perhaps, with its pagan significance, it was not considered proper.

The day before Harvest Festival troops of children and their parents could be seen dropping off produce at the church and volunteers decorated the side windows and the area around the pulpit with a wealth of wonders. The smells began to waft and mingle; fresh picked apples and pears, green smells from the outdoors, the earthy smell of potatoes newly dug from the ground, all commingling into the fragrance that can only be called Harvest. But the best was yet to come.

Harvest Sunday was usually a warm, sunny day, in my remembrance, although we could have had a few early storms. As we walked into the packed church, there, taking center stage, was the biggest loaf of bread you could imagine. Golden brown, it usually took the shape of a sheaf of wheat surrounded by ears of grain. Actual wheat sheaves had been brought in, as well as bales of hay, and all the produce filled the stage in front of the pulpit to overflowing. This tradition probably had its origins way back in pagan history but today this was a Christian tradition. The smells and sounds were overpowering and wonderful. There were cabbages, cauliflowers, potatoes, parsnips, swedes, and onions, loaves of homemade bread, jars of pickles, chutneys and jams, and bottled fruits, apples, plums and pears, jars of jam of every flavor, and even the occasional, prize vegetable marrow. There were flowers too, chrysanthemums from pale golden-yellow to deep russet, the orange bell seeds of the honesty plant, and late blooming roses. There were sprays of colored leaves of every hue from probably every tree in Shirehampton Woods. There were even boughs of horse chestnut complete with their wonderful, green seed cases, and prickly bramble strands. Flanking this wealth of produce were stacked tins of fruits, vegetables, meats, and fish.

We knew that the produce would be shared with the local poor, but we prided ourselves that we had enough not to need the abundance in the church. Dad had work: it didn't pay much but we didn't have to worry where our next meal was coming from. There were special hymns: we sang with gusto *We Plough the Fields and Scatter the Good Seed on the Land* and *Come, Ye Thankful People, Come.* The sermon was usually on the topics of abundance, charity, and thankfulness. We left the church with a rosy glow, not only in our cheeks but in our hearts.

## THE CHIMNEY SWEEP

As the colder winds of October began to blow, Mum and Dad would order in our coal supplies. The coal man would carry in the heavy, hundredweight sacks of coal on his shoulders, one by one, and tip them with a loud crash into our coal shed. Our coal shed, at that time, was an old WWII Anderson air raid shelter that had been re-erected close to the house. Made of curved sections of corrugated iron, its rusted roof made an ideal look-out in our games of pirates and sea-going expeditions.

As soon as the last delivery of coal was settled, I would hurry out to the shed to look for fossils. The glistening, black coal would often reveal the shapes of prehistoric ferns. Mum would never let me keep these specimens in the house, but I made a little collection behind the coal shed. That is, until the end of the winter, when supplies were getting low, and I had to sacrifice my little collection to warm the house. When we had used up the last of the coal, we would trundle an old pram down to Portbury Dock and buy a couple of extra sacks. Sometimes we would get coke, pre-burned coal, but it never gave the same warmth as coal. It never ceased to amaze me that we were burning rocks!

"Drawing up the fire" was a chore that fell to me as I got older. I learned how to crumple the newspapers and add a commercial firelighter to get it started. On top were laid small pieces of chopped wood and then lumps of coal. A double page of the Evening Post was draped across the fireplace with just enough space at the bottom to draw up a draft. What a great and ancient thrill to start a fire and get it roaring up the chimney!

Once a year, before the fires were lit, we had in the chimney sweep. The sweep didn't have far to come as he was our neighbor, a few houses up, Mr. Fred Lloyd. He had a job down on the docks, but he was also a terrific chimney sweep. Before he came, there would be a scurry of activity as we pulled back the chairs from the small, living room fireplace, and covered the furniture with old sheets.

Mr. Lloyd would have already been to several other houses, so he would arrive covered in soot. Mum would lay newspapers down for him to walk on and Mr. Lloyd would bring a tarpaulin, which he draped over the fireplace. We were warned to "Let him work in peace" but we were too excited to watch him string the poles together and shove the round brush up the chimney. We shot multitudes of questions at him. "What if you hit a bird?" and "Do you think there is treasure up there?" We imagined that some previous owner had hidden a box of jewels up the chimney and one day the brush would bring it down.

Finally, we were instructed to go outside and to call when we saw the brush emerge from the top of the chimney. I'm sure that Mr. Lloyd could tell this from the inside, but it got us out of the house and out from under his feet. The brush would emerge, in a cloud of soot, and we would yell "It's out, it's out!" and rush back into the house to see Mr. Lloyd retracting the rods and sweeping up the fallen, sticky, black soot. The soot would be spread on the back garden to provide nutrients for the next summer's vegetable crop. Mr. Lloyd had another job too, providing "good luck" for new brides. At village weddings Mr. Lloyd would come with his brushes to shake the bride's hand. It was a superstition that this would bring good fortune to the marriage.

One year, Mum thought she would save money and bought some firecrackers called Black Imps that claimed to clean the chimney. Mum put newspapers around the fireplace, lit a firecracker, and threw it up the chimney. Bang! Down came clouds of soot and dust, all over the living room. We spent the rest of the day cleaning! Next year, we called in Mr. Lloyd again!

## BONFIRE NIGHT

Bonfire Night, also called Guy Fawkes Night, falls on November 5th every year. It celebrates the thwarting of a 1605 plot to blow up the London Houses of Parliament with barrels of gunpowder and to kill King James 1st. A group of thirteen men stored thirty-six barrels of gunpowder in the cellars of the Houses of Parliament. One of them had second thoughts and wrote a letter warning the King. The cellars were raided and Guy Fawkes, who was down there at the time, got arrested and horribly executed. Bonfires were set alight, on the night of Guy Fawkes' arrest, to proclaim that the King was safe.

We learned this history in school but to us Guy Fawkes Night meant fireworks. Bonfire Night started weeks before November 5th, with rubbish dumps being raided for old wooden furniture, branches and logs were dragged to back gardens, and old wooden crates were added to the growing piles of debris. Newspapers were stuffed in around the base and an old chair was fastened to the top of each towering bonfire. We prayed that it wouldn't rain before Bonfire Night.

We got busy, too, making a Guy Fawkes dummy from old clothes stuffed with newspapers and straw. A paper face was bought or, more often, a crude face was painted onto a piece of cloth, to represent Guy Fawkes. One of Dad's old peaked caps was placed atop the Guy's head. We begged or borrowed pushchairs and carts and paraded our Guys around the streets, begging for "A Penny for the Guy!"

The best place was outside the Coop store up in Shire or near Baldocks, the newspaper shop. Of course, we were in competition with all the other village kids who had made Guys, so we sometimes pooled our resources and shared pitches. "You can have Baldocks in the morning, and we'll put our Guy there in the afternoon." There seemed to be a Guy on every corner. Most people gave us a penny, sometimes more if we had a good Guy, which looked like we had put some effort into our creation.

The pennies added up and, I'm afraid, we spent most of it on sweets. Dad bought most of the fireworks although we did splurge on sparklers and bangers. It was agony waiting for dark to come on Bonfire Night and a few impatient neighbors would set off early rockets. Mum made us put on coats, gloves, scarves and wooly hats before we were allowed outdoors. Our black and white dog, Spot, and Tiny, the black cat, were secured safely indoors. We got busy hauling our Guy up on top the bonfire and searching the bottom of the stack to make sure that no hedgehogs had made their nests there. After setting off a few test rockets, Dad got his matches and started setting blaze to the bonfire. We could have been little Celtic pagans as we danced around the fire. The flames leapt up and quickly devoured the stuffed Guy sitting on the top, to our shouts of "Burn, burn!" The bonfire would quickly die down and Dad would replenish the blaze with broken furniture until everything was gone.

Then came the fireworks; Dad oversaw this operation, too. Catherine wheels would be nailed to the clothes-line posts, rockets would be launched from milk bottles, and bangers placed under a tin washing tub for a more effective explosion. The sky was ablaze with rockets and reflected fire from the many garden bonfires. The smell of cordite hung in the night air, along with the tang of burned wood. Mum would have hot cocoa ready for us indoors, sometimes she would bake potatoes and a gingerbread cake called parkin. We were all "bonfired" out and ready to shed our fire-scented clothes for our warm pajamas.

## CHRISTMAS CAROLING

Fa-la-la-la-la, la-la, la-la! A few weeks before Christmas, with pocket money sparse and the prospect of buying presents looming, Alan and I would start carol singing. We both could hold a good tune and sang lustily in Sunday School. We figured we would do OK going around the houses for some extra money. First, we borrowed a hymn book from Nana Win and asked Dad for fresh batteries for our torches. We practiced a bit before we went out but usually, we just winged it. Sometimes, one of our friends, Angela from next door or Valerie, from across the street, would come with us but, we figured, we would do better financially on our own.

Wrapped up warmly, our first stops would be to relatives in the village: Nana Win and Grampy Jim's, and then on to Aunty Marge and Uncle Arthur's. They were guaranteed to give us sixpence. Most people wanted to hear more than one carol: so, we had a repertoire including *Away in a Manger, O Little Town of Bethlehem, The Holly and the Ivy, We Three Kings of Orient Are, Ding Dong Merrily on High, and While Shepherds Watched their Flocks by Night*. We would start off with *Away in a Manger* and we took it from there until someone would shout "Mum says go away!" or they opened the door and gave us a couple of pennies. We got more pennies than requests to go away. We also knew not to start too early in the season and not to carol sing too close to Christmas, when everyone was getting besieged with carol singers. We also learned early on that the poorest houses gave the most and the richer houses gave less. It was better to visit lots of houses in our neighborhood and we were probably safer, too, as most people knew us.

We had some funny times. We usually didn't sing at houses that had no lights on but, if there was a glimmer of light, there was a glimmer of hope. At one house we started singing, and the drains started gurgling beside us, we sang some more, and the drains gurgled some more. We sang, the drains gurgled. We couldn't sing for laughing. There were also sad times: a mother coming to the door in threadbare clothes, with multiple little children round her ankles. She didn't have any money to give us – but we sang carols for her anyway.

It didn't occur to us to sing and give the money to charity—we were the charity, in our own eyes. All the local children sang carols around the houses and we were no different. Mum and Dad would give us a time to come home, or to return whenever we got too cold, whichever came first. Nana and Grampy usually gave us a cup of warm tea, to see us on our way, and we knew that a hot supper of soup and crusty bread would be waiting at home.

## THE PANTOMIME

As we got closer to Christmas, Dad's company would give the workers tickets to the annual pantomime at the Bristol Hippodrome. This old theater was situated at Bristol Center on St. Augustine's Parade. Historically this area was on the banks of the Frome River with a view of tall-masted sailing ships and bustling port activities. After World War II, the river had been sealed beneath a modern park with roads circulating where the river once ran.

The Hippodrome once had a fanciful frontage with a large globe sitting on top, a retractable roof, and special effects such as a wave tank, which were later removed. To us kids this was a fairyland of red, velvet curtains, excitement and magic. We couldn't imagine a royal palace so large and so beautifully decorated. Dressed in our party best, and after a substantial tea, we rode the bus up to town.

Private boxes and balconies soared above our heads as we claimed our seats in the lower rows. The lights dimmed, the music rose to a crescendo, and the curtains parted to reveal a dazzling, colorful depiction of a country village. Bright and cheerful dancers skipped out in twos and threes to sing the opening numbers to the pantomime. The format was always the same and the pantomime always opened the same way.

Soon, the audience was introduced to the main characters. Male leads, such as Puss in Boots and the Prince in Cinderella, were always played by female characters and female lead roles were filled by men. I'm sure they found the ugliest of men to play the roles of Cinderella's Ugly Sisters! The Dame was usually played by a famous male comedian, such as Tommy Cooper with "a gag a minute". The theme was always a fairy tale such as Babes in the Wood, Jack and the Bean Stalk, or Sleeping Beauty.

The parts that I loved best were when the audience was invited to participate in singing bawdy songs and encouraged to shout out where the "bad" character was hiding, "He's behind you! Look behind you!" we all yelled.

The colorful costumes, the story, the songs, the lights and the music, the jokes, the audience involvement, and the inevitable finale with a ball scene, I loved it all. The pantomime was raw and crude, certainly not politically-correct as in today's cautious over-protection of children's sensibilities. But it did us no harm. We didn't hear anything new at the pantomime that we didn't hear on the street corner or down the pub off-license. It was all part of growing up.

## FATHER CHRISTMAS

This may sound irreverent, but I remember Christmas at Shirehampton Baptist Church not for the Christmas services but for the appearance of Father Christmas. On the day of the Sunday School Christmas Party Mum would pick out small china plates, bowls, and spoons for Alan and me. According to instructions, sent home the previous Sunday, she would attach a piece of colored wool onto each piece so that we would bring the same dishes home!

We dressed in our winter Sunday clothes which for me were a tartan, plaid dress with a home-knit wool cardigan. Alan wore short trousers, even in winter, with long socks up to his knees, and a warm, wooly sweater, that had been knitted by Mum. We knew that there would be an afternoon feast waiting for us at the Sunday School. The party was held in the old, tar paper and plywood Sunday School hut, at the back of the Baptist Church, on Station Road. It was heated by a black pot-bellied, coal-burning stove that seemed huge to me as a child. Cradle Roll posters and religious pictures were decorated with colorful, paper chains and silver stars, made from tinfoil, for the party.

Before the Christmas Party began, we played games: Oranges and Lemons, Ring a Ring O' Roses, and The Farmers in the Dell. This not only sharpened our appetites but burned off a lot of energy so, by the time we sat at the folding tables, we were relatively quiet and ready to eat.

What a banquet: jelly and blancmange, Scotch eggs, custards, cakes, and puddings all made by the Mums and church staff. There was milky, sweet tea, as well as a watery, orange drink. We ate as if we hadn't eaten for months, although our mums had given us a good dinner before we left home.

Next, came the part that I liked the best. A Christmas tree sat in one corner of the room and we were all guided to sit cross-legged on the wood floor and listen to a Christmas story while the adults cleared away the party debris. The older kids were drafted, too, to help sweep the floor, and take down the tables. It was getting quite dark by now as the afternoon wore on.

Then, a hush came over the room as the lights were dimmed. We all sat cross legged around the Christmas tree and were told to listen! We were listening for Father Christmas's bell. At first there was nothing and a few of us started to fidget. I was never good at sitting. Then….ting, ting, ting! Seemingly coming from a long way away came the sound of a hand bell. We gasped and whispered to each other, "He's coming!" The ringing came closer and closer and one of the mums would get up to open the outside door.

In a rush of cold air in came Father Christmas with a large sack over his shoulder. I remember the magical feeling that would come over me: a bit scared as this large man entered with a hearty "Ho, ho, ho" and anticipation at what he would bring me!

Father Christmas would stride to a chair, put out for him by one of the staff, who acted deferentially, as if he really was Father Christmas. "Sit here, Father Christmas, so all the children can see you." One by one our names were read out and we all received a present. He asked us if we had been good, which of course we said we had. Who was going to risk not getting a present?

I often wondered who paid for all the gifts as we all got something nice: a painting set, a coloring book, or a game. When all the presents had been given out, Father Christmas would explain that he still had a lot of work to do and had to be going. With another "Ho, ho, ho" and another draft of cold air, he was gone. The lights came on, we got our coats and scarves and party plates, and the little ones started looking for their mums and dads who were coming to get them. Alan and I walked home, back to Meadow Grove, glowing and full of Christmas happiness, jelly, pudding and cake.

## THE CHRISTMAS PILLOW CASE

I would always awake very, very early on Christmas morning. The street lights still shone through the frost-encrusted windows making fern patterns inside the glass panes. We had no heat upstairs. Reluctant to rise from my warm, flannel-sheeted bed I would reach down to the bottom with my foot to feel the heaviness of the Christmas Pillowcase. I called out to my brother "Did he come yet?" meaning, of course, Father Christmas. Rustling of wrapping paper told me Alan had already started opening his presents. Reaching sideways out of bed, I would grab my woolen dressing gown, pull it inside the covers and put it on before throwing back the bedclothes to reveal The Pillowcase.

Wrapping myself in my quilt, I usually reached out for the first, large shape inside the Pillowcase. As always, Nana Tanzell had dressed a large doll in totally hand-knitted baby clothes. I hugged the doll as a "Thank-you" to Nana. Some Christmases she dressed one of my Aunty Sylvia's old dolls and handed them down to me for tender loving care. This year I could tell it was a new one with soft, white clothing. You could never tell what color Nana would use to knit the doll's clothes. Sometimes they were pink, sometimes blue, one year a wild, lime-green, it all depended on what knitting wool she had left over. Tucking the doll into bed, I would reach for the rest of the Pillowcase.

First, I would smell the presents. Some would smell of Devon Violet toiletries a fragrance I hated, and still dislike. These would be put aside. Others smelled of chocolate and toffee and I opened these first. Our parents with their ever-present radar would call out "Don't eat any sweets before breakfast!" This was totally disregarded, and a gauzy Christmas stocking would be ripped open and Mars Bars, Crunchies, and other assorted chocolate bars would fall out.

Great wonders came out of the Christmas Pillowcase: plastic brush and comb sets, books with exciting titles like Little Women and Black Beauty, lengths of hair ribbon, more sweets, flat tins of toffee with little metal hammers, painting sets, coloring books, children's games, more books (because everybody knew I liked to read). We were supposed to save the tags, so that mum and dad would know who gave us what, but all that was left at the end were three piles: one of wrapping paper, a second of presents, and a third of rejected gifts like socks and Devon Violet toiletries.

Next came the swapping. My brother would bring all his presents, including rejects, into my bedroom. Pulling back the heavy curtains we had enough winter light to compare gifts and do some early trading. I got all my brother's books and extra paint sets and he got some of my games and toffee tins. We did this before our parents were even up. Later, they would be puzzled why I had received Treasure Island and Robinson Crusoe, surely books for boys! When we were younger, we had to wait in bed until our parents decided to get up. That was probably why we got the Christmas Pillowcases on the end of the bed, to keep us busy for an hour or so. But, as we got older, we could go quietly downstairs, where our main presents were stacked on the dining table. Mine on one side and my brother's on the other. There were games that were too large for the Pillowcases, more painting sets, coloring books, and magic sets, enough to keep two children occupied all through Christmas Day and Boxing Day.

## CHRISTMAS DAY

Christmas Day usually turned out to be a cold, frosty day with a spot of warm, sunshine in the afternoon. After checking that Father Christmas had drunk the small glass of dry sherry, that Mum and Dad had left him the night before, we started opening our presents. We would come downstairs, in our wooly dressing gowns and slippers, where our presents were laid out on the table. Mum and Dad would light a coal fire in the grate and put the kettle on the stove for a morning cup of tea. We received board games, Christmas annuals, painting sets, coloring books, magic tricks, stenciling sets, and more books.

With a hot pot of tea on the table, amid the mounds of ripped wrapping paper, Mum and Dad would open the presents that we had bought them with our pocket and carol singing money. We gave Dad shiny, springy suspenders to hold up his shirt sleeves, a pristine white hankie set, folded in a flat, white box and embroidered with his initial R, a new pair of slippers (that we bought with Mum's financial help) and a jar of Brylcream for his hair. Mum delighted in her flower-embroidered handkerchiefs, a bottle of Eau-de-Cologne, a cotton scarf decorated with her favorite irises, and a small box of Cadbury's Black Magic chocolates.

We were usually too excited to eat breakfast, but Mum would threaten to take our toys away for the day, if we didn't eat. Reluctantly, we would sit down for a light breakfast of cooked oatmeal and another cup of tea. Mum drizzled Tate and Lyle's golden syrup over the surface of the porridge to encourage us to eat it all. Before breakfast, Alan and I, territorial as only close siblings can be, stashed our gifts on opposite sides of the living room fireplace. We had already done our swaps and now, what was ours was ours!

Most of what I remember about Christmas Day was eating! We only ate tangerines at Christmas, so they always evoke memories of the holidays. Dad would get out his hammer from his tool box and would carefully crack Brazils and hazelnuts in the fireplace, throwing the shells onto the coals, where they would spit and pop. We played Ludo, Snap, and Snakes and Ladders in front of the fire. We would listen to the wireless which usually had some good carols playing from Bristol Cathedral. Near noon, we would get dressed in our Sunday clothes, brush our teeth, and wash our faces, ready for Christmas Dinner. This would be at relatives or at our own house.

When we provided Christmas Dinner, it was usually a large, roast chicken or duck with all the fixings: stuffing, roast and boiled potatoes, parsnips, Brussels sprouts, and delicious Bisto gravy made in the roasting pan. Dessert was Christmas pudding with hot Bird's custard. And, of course, there would be Christmas Crackers, which we would all take turns pulling with whoever was sitting next to us. Soon, everyone would be wearing colorful, paper hats, reading mottos and jokes, and playing with the tiny toys from the Crackers. Mum would have been cooking all morning, so after lunch the adults would take a nap, while we were cautioned to "Play quietly!" Mid-afternoon, still stuffed from dinner, Mum would gather up the children, any relatives who were at our house, and lots of neighborhood kids to go for a walk. This was traditional on Christmas Day. We trooped up to Penpole Point or down Barracks Lane to feed Dolly the rag-and-bone-man's horse with apples.

# BOXING DAY

Boxing Day, the day after Christmas was a strange day. No other countries seemed to celebrate this day and it was always a bit of an anticlimax after Christmas. It was a day to dress up and visit relatives for another big dinner, this one of roast pork, to play with our presents, and to eat up all the leftovers for supper.

The origins of Boxing Day are obscure and there are many definitions of this odd day. It was said to have originated in the big, wealthy houses of aristocratic England, when Christmas Day belonged to the wealthy family of the house. Staff were not allowed home but served the family during their big parties, balls, and other Christmas celebrations. Boxing Day was the day that the servants received boxes containing new shoes, material for new uniforms, and left-over food. If they were lucky, the servants got a half day off to visit their families. Some big houses held a Servants' Ball where the Master of the House danced with the housemaids and the family members served food to the staff. Boxes containing money and goods were also given to the postman and other trades people on Boxing Day.

Boxing Day was also a day of traditional sports such as fox hunting when most big villages brought out horses, hounds and riders in pink or red riding jackets. Nowadays hunting is banned, and many people watch sports on TV. In our family Boxing Day was a good excuse to get out into the countryside for a long walk in the fresh air, to try and walk off some of the pounds gained over Christmas. Whatever its origins, it was nice to have an extra day off work and school.

## PORTWAY SECONDARY MODERN

Portway School Uniform

In the autumn of 1957, it came time to move to the Secondary School, up in the village. Portway Secondary School was our family's school; that is, my Dad, and aunties on both sides of the family had attended the school. My Mum had been there, too, for a few years, as her family moved around, and it was in Shire that she met Dad.

Dad's "claim to fame" was that he and some of his classmates had wired the school for sound, a sort of early intercom system but it was no longer in use when I started. Both my parents left school at 14 years of age (the required leaving age); Mum to be a housemaid in Bristol and Dad to work at Spillers Flour Mill at Avonmouth.

I was very nervous about leaving the sanctuary of Avon Primary down Barracks Lane. The junior school was very close to our house on Meadow Grove and all my friends went there. Now, many of us would be split up. I didn't quite qualify for the grammar schools as I had failed the second part of the 11-Plus exams that all children took in the last year of junior school. Some of my friends were going to Colston Grammar, Red Maids and other Bristol Grammar schools.

Also, because there were so many of us baby-boomer post-war children there were too many children for one or even two classes and we would be split into at least five different classes during our first year at Portway. I was placed in 1P (the top level of Year One was split into two classes and I was in the parallel class to the top level).

At that time Miss Shewell was the Head Teacher and Miss Dyer, the Deputy Head. Our First-Year class had 40 girls and Miss Harris was our Home Room Teacher. Our average age during the first year was between 11 and 12 years old. At Avon Primary we did most of our work in one classroom with one teacher, now we would have to work with a timetable and move between classrooms for different subjects. This made me very anxious and I wasn't looking forward to the move. But it had to be.

On September 9, 1957, aged 11 years and 4 months I entered the BIG school and stayed there until July 27, 1962. I chose Colston House, as my cousin Christine Barnes recommended it and I eventually became a member of the school orchestra, a school magazine representative, and a lunch monitor.

## PORTWAY – FIRST YEAR

I still have my Portway School report card, a small blue book, and this shows that for the first year, we took thirteen subjects: Holy Scripture, Arithmetic, English, Geography, History, Science, Needlework, Music, Art, Physical Education and French. The first term I got one A, and mostly Bs and Cs. My best subject was needlework and my worst arithmetic! The most common comments were "Tries hard" and "Must work harder", and "Greater effort needed"! Interestingly, I was evaluated as "An imaginative writer – but grammar and spelling rather weak."

What do I remember most from that term? Memories include learning to sew on a treadle sewing machine to make the gingham apron and organza cap that we would wear when we began Domestic Science class the next year. I didn't realize it, at that time, but they were training most of us to be competent house-wives and housekeepers!

Physical Education or PE was often carried out in the back playground, adjoining the Portway, and we had to wear our navy-blue "bloomer" knickers and our white school blouses. The next year we could wear real shorts and Aertex shirts. There was also a sports field further down the Portway where we played cricket (with a hard-wood ball) and field hockey (I played center half, as it wasn't such a dangerous position!)

I also remember Miss Bannister's history class where we had to stand at our rows of traditional desks until the teacher arrived, then she would say "Good Morning Young Ladies" and we could sit. Despite this formality, Miss Bannister was a pleasant teacher and introduced us to the early history of the Shirehampton and Bristol areas. She had us create dioramas of early Saxon villages and families using small dolls.

We also had two years of French with our one male teacher but the whole class, including me, was very disobedient. We did not pay attention, climbed under the desks and switched seats and generally did not do very well. Sadly, he left after our second year.

My favorite memory was the garden that bordered the Portway, a busy road that ran from Bristol to Avonmouth. Crab apple trees grew here and ranged from glorious pink blossoms in the spring to small, red crab apples (that we ate) later in the year. This was a respite from the two busy playgrounds, and we were able to relax and socialize.

Overall, that first year was very stressful but we all made it through and adapted to moving between classrooms for different subjects – but we looked forward to the long school holidays in the summer! Sadly, although I was a B student, I came 38 of 39 in the year-end school exams!

# MAKING MUSIC

Sometime during the second term of the first year we were assembled in the upper assembly hall and told that we could choose a musical instrument to learn to play. The instrument would be provided by the Bristol Education Department and we would be expected to attend classes and to practice.

We already had music lessons that consisted mainly of us sitting in our desks singing folk songs and learning to harmonize. We didn't learn to read music, but we were evaluated, and I was told that I was "pitch perfect" but I had no idea what that was!

In the assembly hall we were introduced to the different instruments that were available: the violin, the viola, and the cello. I didn't want to play the violin; I was unsure about the viola (thinking it was just a bigger violin) and put my hand up to learn to play the cello.

This led to a series of events that made me (almost) want to change my mind. First, although the Education Department supplied the instruments, our parents were expected to eventually pay for them in weekly installments. My Mum was furious and questioned me about how I was expecting to earn a living playing the cello? It seemed that only those efforts towards an eventual career were worth investing in. She even came up the school to talk to the music teacher but, eventually, began sending small weekly payments for my very own cello.

Practice took place first in the small school library and then in the music teacher's classroom during lunch break. Lessons were held every Saturday morning, in an old education building behind the Council House (now called City Hall) at the bottom of Park Street. Instruments were available for us and we were introduced to the basics of playing the cello. I loved the deep tones of the cello and was moderately OK.

Later, I got good enough to play in the Bristol Junior Youth Orchestra that met at a large red-brick school up at St. George in Bristol. I traveled from Shire on the bus with my cello and had many ribald remarks from the bus conductors like "Hey love, how do you get that one under your chin then?"

But I have a confession: I was never able to read music! I realize now that I suffered from a condition known as *dyscalculia*, that also hindered me in learning math and symbolic learning such as shorthand. Fortunately, each new piece was played on the piano by the music teacher and I was able to memorize the cello parts! So, for five years I was able to "wing it" and even played in the school assembly, a small local church group, and with the Bristol Junior Youth Orchestra!

## THE SCHOOL LIBRARY

During 1957, Portway School got its own library! It was carved out of a storage room at the top of the steps that divided the Lower from the Upper School and was very small. There was just enough room for a check-out desk, behind which was a long magazine rack. The rest of the room was taken up with book shelves in a honey-blond wood and a couple of tables and chairs. A window looked down onto the Lower School playground and another small window looked out into the corridor.

Here we learned how to check out books, taking turns each class to be the librarian, learned the Dewey Decimal System and learned how to catalog and restock the shelves. I already knew much of this as I had been borrowing books from the Shire Library since before I went to school.

My choice in books around this time, aged 11, was very juvenile: our neighbors has a television and I gravitated to books such as Bill and Ben the Flowerpot Men and Muffin the Mule. Gradually, I explored other genres, especially travel and biographies and quickly read through a series of books with titles: Children of Japan, Children or Norway, Children of Africa and learned about life in other countries.

I had always been a reader. Before starting school, I was read to by Mum from children's comics and when I began reading for myself, I enjoyed a children's magazine called Sunny Smiles, Toby Twirl, Rupert Bear and others. I remember how Sunny Smiles came about. It was not a children's magazine that you could buy at the newsagents: you had to subscribe. Promoters came to the school and passed out leaflets and a free copy, I took it home and begged my mother to get it for me.

Between classes the school library was kept locked, but I and another pupil could use the room for our cello practice at lunchtime. The other girl was much quicker than me, as I had a problem reading music and I felt quite discouraged. I talked to Miss Powney, our music teacher, and she encouraged me to keep practicing. She explained that everyone progressed at their own pace: some faster or slower than others. Eventually, my music partner dropped out of cello classes and I continued learning and playing until I left school.

One of the magazines stocked in the school library was The New Elizabethan. This was an exciting journal full of post-war discoveries, inventions and novel ideas. One time, they advertised a competition run by Cadburys chocolate that accompanied an article on how chocolate was grown in large pods in tropical lands, harvested and sent by boat to the UK and other countries. There the seeds were roasted, ground, mixed with sugar and milk products and formed into the bars we are familiar with.

The competition asked us to write a short story about chocolate and the prize would be a large collection of chocolate! Of course, I entered but didn't win the big prize. But we all got prizes, a small box of Cadbury's miniature chocolate bars!

## REBELLION!

Most teens, when they reach a certain age, tend to rebel! Some of my classmates and friends began to smoke, copying their parents, some drank alcohol, others shoplifted or joined gangs that vandalized local property. I was a quiet, shy girl and my rebellion took the form of going to church!

At age twelve, I make the decision to leave Shirehampton Baptist Church, where I had been attending, since I was two years old, and joined the newly-opened Pentecostal church up near the Barrow Hill Quarry. I liked the newness of the church, the lively music, the non-traditional services – and I took my younger brother with me!

Mum always expected me to help clean the house on Sunday mornings but now I had an excuse, "Sorry Mum, I have to go to church!" What could she say? I was a stubborn child and decided that, despite the family's disapproval, this would be my choice.

I didn't always go along with the Pentecostal beliefs or behaviors; I didn't "Speak in Tongues" and I was not a "Holy Roller". But. after a few years I was teaching Sunday School to the juniors and even preached from the pulpit on Youth Sundays! I have no idea what I talked about but probably something about loving your neighbors.

I stayed a member of the congregation until I was sixteen when I left school and we moved to Dorset for Dad's work.

# PARIS!

**PALAIS DE VERSAILLES**

In the Third Year at Portway, I had became moderately fluent in French, enough so that I taught my brother some key phrases and words. Our class was offered a chance to visit Paris!

Wow, I was so excited, but my Mum brought me back down to earth. There was very little money available for such luxuries as foreign travel. But, after promising all my pocket money, doing extra jobs around the house, and assuring Mum that we could pay for it in small weekly installments, she relented.

A photo of our group in our summer school uniforms can be seen with us in the courtyard of the Palace of Versailles. I am the shy young woman standing next to our guide, and still have vivid memories of that trip.

The smell of coffee takes me back to the *pension*, the small tourist hotel on the Rue du Faubourg, I don't remember the District. A *pension* is a type of guest house or boarding house and the term is used on the Continent. *Pensions* are usually historic buildings, are often family-run, and are generally cheaper than other lodging.

We could go down to the coffee shop on the corner and drink coffee (for the first time in my life) with our holiday money and without teacher supervision. It was one of the first emancipating moments of my life.

The *pension* was tiny, with many floors and only a couple of rooms on each floor. The rooms had several beds and a small cubicle to wash, including a *bidet*! We had no idea what this was for until a teacher explained.

As we entered the building, we were often greeted by the family and allowed to peek into their kitchen, that had a very large bathtub in the middle of the room! The whole *pension* smelled deliciously of brewed coffee!

There were probably rats or mice in the building, as I was often kept awake with scratching under my bed, that I thought were ghosts. There were probably both!

During the week we visited the beautiful Sacre-Coeur church (where we had to cover our hair with a handkerchief to enter), Montmartre with its flower sellers and bookstalls, a countryside food market (where I bought "stinky" cheese for Dad), boated down the Seine, marveled at the Rose Window in Notre Dame Cathedral, and walked for miles around the Palais of Versailles and the Petit Trianon.

Our lunches were huge *baguettes* filled with meats and cheeses that we hungry teenagers wolfed down. Our evening meal was in a real restaurant, drinking water-down red wine, the best vegetable soups I had ever tasted and "mystery" meats, one of which we were told was "frogs' legs", but I still like to think they were joking.

## THE CEMETERY

As kids, we had no fear of death, only a great curiosity. We knew, from an early age that people died, and we had to live without them. We learned that our little brother, Michael, had died when he was a toddler from influenza pneumonia that was widespread in post-war England. Our Great-Grandparents, Granny and Grampy Saunders also had graves in the Shirehampton cemetery.

Every couple of weeks, Mum would pick flowers from our garden in Meadow Grove and visit Shirehampton Cemetery. This was an education as we would wander around and read the tombstone inscriptions.

The gates were always unlocked, vandalism was rare, and we could even visit the cemetery without our parents. As we entered, we would pick up a metal watering can and fill it with water from the trough. We knew where our little brother's grave was in the small graveyard.

We would empty out the dead flowers from the vases and arrange fresh flowers, along with little "chats" about what a "lovely day" it was.

Michael's grave had a small oblong headstone and a grave about the size of a child's bed, filled with dirt, that was later covered with green stones. Nearby, were the simple graves of Granny and Grampy Saunders, each a simple concrete rectangle filled with green plants. An inscription along the edges gave the names, dates of birth and death: very simple. They had both died in their 90s!

The graveyard was well-kept, and we often met a workman with a push-mower and even, sometimes, one with a scythe, an ancient metallic curved blade on a long handle, that was historically used to cut grass and crops.

The cemetery was always quiet, except for the ocassional car going by and birdsong. The trees were probably ancient, and I wondered about the houses that backed onto the graveyard. Did they ever see ghosts?

# JOURNALISM

Since being a little girl, I loved to write; poetry, short stories and I even started an unofficial school newsletter, each copy hand-written and sold for one penny! The newsletter didn't last long but I was left with a longing to write. I helped with the official school newspaper that, I think, came out twice a year, and had my poetry published there. My dream was to be a journalist.

My mother knew this and arranged for me to meet a local woman journalist who lived in a house over at Pill. Her large house, The Watch House, that looked out over the River Avon, seemed wonderful to me as a youngster raised in a red-brick council house.

The journalist, Barbara Buchanan, had a weekly column in the Bristol Evening Post, that was very popular. My Mum got her number from the newspaper and phoned her up asking for a meeting so that I could talk to her about journalism. She very graciously agreed!

So, Mum and I took the ferry over to Pill and walked the short distance up to her house. She was kind and generous with her time. Instead of her formal office she ushered us into a small sitting room, and we sat at a polished table overlooking her garden. Her advice was both encouraging and disheartening. She told me about the difficulties of finding a journalism job and advised me to stay in school and write as often as I could, and I would one day be a professional writer. She was right! Thank you, Barbara!

## DOMESTIC SCIENCE

One of my favorite classes was domestic science. There were two domestic science kitchens, one in the Upper school and one in the Lower school. Both were fully equipped; they even had a washing machine and ovens. And each had an attached replica of a living/dining room where we learned to clean and served cooked lunches to our invited friends.

We didn't begin cooking classes until the second year at Portway and began with very easy dishes: stewed pears with custard, shortbread biscuits, and savory mince. We became more and more adventurous over the years and eventually prepared and cooked: soups, sauces, meat dishes, fish, vegetable dishes, flans and cakes of all kinds, puddings and pies, egg dishes, jams and jellies, pastry dishes of all kinds even hot-crust pastry game pie which was quite difficult.

All the girls made the same dish and after lunch they were displayed on a center table for the approval of the DS teacher! There was everything from total flops to rising masterpieces! I had my share of both. One year we made Christmas cakes, baking the actual cake one week, then icing it the next. I decided to make one that I had seen in a magazine, where you cut half a layer off the top so there is a step down and then iced the whole thing, so it looked like a snowy slope. I bought cake decorations: a little boy in a bunny suit on a sled, a little skier, and small trees. It looked lovely, especially with the ever-needed Christmas paper band around it.

The first year we had a DS teacher who scared me (I don't remember her name, I wonder why?) The second year we had our beloved Mrs. Fowles: The first class with her she announced: "My name may be Fowles, but I am no chicken and I have the eyes and ears of a hawk!" We totally respected her, and she took us on many culinary adventures. She once asked if I thought my family would eat a carrot flan! I told her my Dad would probably throw it out! Those classes taught me many valuable lessons that have helped me all my life!

# EARLY TEENS

The early teens brought new responsibilities! There were no age limits (that we knew about anyway) preventing young teens from doing many of the activities that adults pursued, such as smoking and going to the pub.

Once I began domestic science at Portway Secondary Mum went to work in the evenings at Peak Freen's biscuit factory down Avonmouth. She also cleaned houses during the day, so everyone was expected to pitch-in. Dad had a series of day jobs, at the Smelting Works, PhilBlack's (carbon black), and Fison's (fertilizer).

My main job was to look after my younger brother from the time Mum went to work until Dad got home and cook dinner for the family. I was twelve years old at the time. Dad was not happy that Mum was working so he always made a fuss about the meal that it "wasn't like Mum made it!" The meals were simple, and Mum sometimes made the main dish beforehand like a shepherd's pie, but Dad was never happy. So, I lied! I told him that Mum had cooked the meal and we kept it warm for him. He seemed happier but like most men of that era he never said, "Thank you."

Pre-teen and teenagers were also expected to run errands, like picking up something from the local shops, pay the paper bills, or get some cigarettes for Mum. Dad smoked heavily and rolled his own cigarettes from Golden Virginia tobacco. Mum smoked Woodbines that she bought five at a time at Baldock's paper shop.

Other errands took us over to a neighbor's house to place a bet for Mum on the football pools, to the pub to pay Dad's union dues, or to pick up a bottle of cider at the pub off-license window. We were kept busy and out of mischief!

# DATING

My parents were strict, even though my Mum first met and dated my Dad when she was 16yrs old. They got engaged before he was sent off to fight in France during the Second World War and she waited five years for his return.

I didn't date until we had moved down to Dorset when I was almost 17, and even then, it was only a "holding hands, peck on the cheek" dating with a local young man. I wanted to date but was a quiet, shy young woman and I wasn't allowed to go to the Bristol coffee houses or discos, that were the rage then.

Instead, I "invented" a boyfriend, Stuart, who I wrote about in a little journal I was keeping. It was pure fantasy and fun until my Mum read the diary! What I wrote was very innocent, teenage imagination and ponderings. When I explained, she thought it was all very silly and told me I had plenty of time for "all that" when I was older!

In contrast, most of my classmates were already dating and at least two of them got pregnant during their fourth year at Portway. As several of the teachers also got pregnant and weren't married, this added to the classroom gossip.

Naturally, I had *crushes* but that was the limit of my romantic adventures. Perhaps it would have been better to begin dating while I was younger as, when I did seriously date in my 20s, I met and married an older, divorced man for all the wrong reasons.

It was the first time I had ever experienced violence from the hands of another person. I appreciate that my parents shielded me from the darker sides of life, but I was ill prepared for adult life.

# THE PRINCESS DRESS

Mum knitted almost all our wooly jumpers and Nana Win knitted all our socks. Mum also had a trusty, hand-cranked Singer sewing machine and she made some of our clothes by-hand. While we were growing, we often had hand-me-downs from neighbor families and from jumble sales. As we got older, we could choose clothes from a Marshall Ward's catalog, and we went up to St. Paul's to buy shoes on credit from Grimes shoe shop. It was rare that we got anything brand new or fashionable.

Most of our daily clothes were Portway's school uniform, that consisted of either a navy-blue gym slip, a type of sleeveless overdress that buttoned at the shoulders, worn with a white shirt, school tie, white socks and sensible shoes. One of Mum's jumpers or cardigans was worn in the winter. In summer school rules were relaxed and we could wear a navy pleated skirt with a white shirt or a sleeved dress of blue and white check material. The tie was in the school colors of blue and gold and we wore elastic tabs to keep up our socks with the school colors. I wore green tabs for Colston.

In sewing classes at school, after making the required domestic science apron and cap in the first year, we were instructed in how to sew real clothes. I first made a cotton skirt with a Tyrolean dancers design on it, then baby doll pajamas, followed by a Kelly-green dress with a boat line neck and narrow waist, that I wore in a school fashion show. During the fifth year, I assisted with the school play and other productions by sewing the costumes.

As well as learning how to sew we also learned to smock, darn, quilt, set in sleeves and zippers, create plackets for buttons, make buttonholes, create different size pleats for skirts, form shapes for different necklines and collars for dresses and blouses, and many other types of dressmaking skills. We also learned how to "turn a sheet". This was Post War England and frugality was valued. So, if a sheet became worn it could be cut down the middle, turned and sewn with a flat French seam, so that the sides became the middle, creating a new sheet!

When I was around fifteen, Mum surprised me by saying that Dad wanted to buy me something nice to wear! He had never expressed any interest in our clothes except when we got grubby. So, one Saturday we bussed up to town and shopped around. And there it was! The most gorgeous, dark-blue brocade dress; embroidered with tiny flowers, cap sleeves, wide skirt to the knees and rounded neckline. I tried it on and felt like a princess.

Dad bought it for me! I felt loved and appreciated, as I knew it cost a lot. This gave me a new appreciation for nice things.

Around that time American magazines were very popular in England and I loved the fashions, especially the coat dresses. These were shirt-waist dresses with another skirt partly concealed underneath but looking as if the outer dress was like a small coat. It seemed so fashionable then and I wanted one so badly. Unfortunately, by the time I emigrated to the US in 1981, the style had gone out of fashion.

It was a different time! It wasn't until I left school that I wore stockings and I even wore a girdle for a short time when I left school. But, being a modern young woman, I soon decided things for myself and wore clothes that I either bought or made for myself!

## THE FIFTH YEAR

At the beginning of the 4th Year at Portway, we were advised that those of us who wanted to stay on and take the Union of Educational Institutes (UEI) examinations could decide to stay for a 5th Year. I was excited at the prospect. But when I voiced the option to my parents, they were not happy with the idea. Although Mum and Dad both worked there was not a lot of income and it was expected that the children would leave school and work to supplement the family budget. It was also expected that, until old enough to become independent, my brother and I would give our weekly pay to our parents and we would be given an allowance for bus fares, lunches, stockings and a small amount of personal money.

I decided to reason with them, after all I was all of fifteen! My reason was that with an extra year of typing and shorthand I would be able to get a better job when I left school. And, they agreed with me, and decided to let me stay the extra year!

At the end of the 4$^{th}$ year when many of my friends were leaving, I was preparing for a 5$^{th}$ year at Portway. Our class 5G now had 21 students for the final term, compared to 40 at the start of the 1$^{st}$ year. Our Home Room Teacher was Mrs. Kinloch and she treated us as adults, rather than children!

Most of us were scheduled to take several UEI examinations, the secondary school leaving certificate, during the year, and some were entered to take the General Certificate Examinations (GCE). I asked but was told that my school work was not up to that standard and I would remain on the UEI Exam list.

We had a great deal of free-study time, and after exams, we had even more free time. We were not allowed to leave until the end of the 5$^{th}$ year but we were found activities to keep us busy. I enjoyed needlework, so I volunteered to make costumes for a live chess game that the 4$^{th}$ year were putting on. Students in costume would move around a giant board in the playground according to two students who were playing the game.

We also had time to hang out in the warmer weather in the apple orchard, bordering the Portway, discussing every subject under the sun.

Mrs. Kinloch also introduced us to the art of debate and dialogue, which stood me in good stead in later life.

    I continued to practice and play the cello, and played at school assembly, our church group, and with the Bristol Junior Youth Orchestra. But all good things come to an end and the transition to work was not an easy one. I had hoped my parents would let me have one more summer at home but, no, I was expected to leave school and get right to work! At sixteen years and a few months I was thrust out into the working world!

## JOB HUNTING

I finally left Portway Girls on July 27, 1962 aged 16 years. Most of my friends had left a year earlier at 15 but I stayed the extra year, which I am glad I did. I was hoping that my parents would let me have one last summer at home before I had to get a job. It was very daunting to realize that I would be working 9 to 5, probably in an office, and would not have the freedom I did before. My parents were not happy about me staying home for the summer as they needed the extra income. They told me that I needed to get a full-time job as soon as possible! I went straight from school to working.

In my Portway School Record is a Leaving Certificate signed by Miss Draper, the Head Mistress who wrote, "Angela has spent a good Fifth Year. She is a hard-working, reliable girl." And Mrs. Kinloch, my Form Teacher had written "Angela has completed her fifth year with very satisfactory results. She is studious and hard-working." And "A serious, hardworking girl who shows intelligence." My Best Subjects were noted as English, Domestic Science and Needlework!

Before the leaving date, my Mother had visited with the Head Mistress to discuss my future! I was not invited to this meeting. The Head suggested that I would be suited for a job as a housekeeper or cook! My mother didn't think this would be good for me, but they were needing my income, and anything would be OK, according to my mother.

Then, we all had to have an interview with a "career counselor" and I told her that I wanted to be a journalist. She laughed at the suggestion and told me that I was matched to work at a stocking factory that was opening in Avonmouth. Shocked, and stubborn as usual, I told her I would look for my own job.

Dad insisted that I get on my bike and cycle down to Avonmouth and ask at the local companies such as the Port of Bristol Authority (PBA), Fison's (fertilizer factory), and PhilBlack (carbon black manufacturer), if they had openings for a secretary/clerk. I was too shy to do that. Fortunately, one of the Portway teachers decided to act as a job counselor and pointed me to two potential job openings. Ironically, one of them was at Fison's and the other up in Bristol; Roneo Corporation, one of the first manufacturers and sellers of photocopiers. I passed the Fison's test and interview and made it to the short-list, but the Roneo job sounded more interesting.

Half a dozen of us were interviewed for the Roneo job (this was post WWII with lots of eligible youngsters) and, amazingly, I got the position. The job was as a junior clerk: typing, filing, making coffee, and other support jobs from 9 a.m. to 5 p.m. I remember the first day as feeling like it was the longest day of my life!

After I had been there for a bit, I made friends with the other staff and the young salesmen, learned the PBX phone system, and didn't mind the Number 28 bus ride from Shire, in and out of Bristol Center. The skills I had learned at school and this first employment gave me a good base for many future jobs and education.

My first job gave me a bit more independence and freedom, even though I had to hand over my weekly pay to my mother and she gave me an allowance for bus fares, nylons, lunches and other personal items. But working opened up a whole new world!

# MOVING!

Dad had worked at several different jobs at Avonmouth: Fison's, PhilBlacks, and the Smelting Works, but he never seemed happy. We got perks! When he was at PhilBlacks, the workers were provided with new towels, bars of Palmolive soap and other commodities and these came home to us. Dad took our old towels to work as replacements. Mum also worked at Peak Freen's biscuit factory and brought home paper bags of broken biscuits that were sold cheaply to the employees.

Dad heard about a scheme where tenants in Council housing could swap with each other, regardless of the county in which they lived. We had always gone down to Dorset for a week in the summer holidays: to a caravan at Swannage, a holiday rental in Bournemouth, or staying with relatives at Poole. So, it seemed natural to try there. Dad put a newspaper ad in the Bournemouth Echo and got several replies.

By this time, he was working at Filton airfield as a Fitters Mate, assisting the mechanical engineers. One job in Dorset sounded interesting: as a Fitters Mate at Hurn Airport (now Bournemouth Airport). The family there wanted to relocate to Bristol so their Dad could work at Filton.

Mum and Dad were delighted but the news came in the middle of my fifth year at Portway School and I wanted to finish out the year. Eventually, they were able to negotiate with the other family and delay the move until the end of the year, so that I could finish school and get some job experience. This was a relief, but I felt very anxious about leaving our extended family in Shire and moving to a completely new life.

## A NEW LIFE

My first job after Portway was at Roneo (Gestetner – a German company, one of the first photocopier sales firms). I had just turned 16 at the end of April and started my new job a week or so after leaving school in the July of 1962. Even having Cs in typing and shorthand, I was hired as a junior clerk. The offices were in a converted warehouse that was reputed to be haunted, opposite the Colston Hall at the Center.

I enjoyed being part of a busy office and meeting new people, but the days dragged. I would get up early to catch the 28 bus up to Bristol City Center and, by the autumn it was getting dark when I left to catch the bus home.

Many of my classmates had left the year earlier, as 15 was the official school leaving age, and they found jobs with the Port of Bristol Authority (PBA), department stores, like Woolworths, and smaller offices. We were some of the first Baby Boomers to look for work and there was a lot of competition for jobs.

It was not hard work at Roneo: filing, a bit of typing on one of the first electric typewriters, keeping tabs of mail and making teas for the two breaks: one mid-morning and one mid-afternoon. We took breaks upstairs near one of the other departments and I enjoyed the new friends I made.

However, the time had come for the family to move down to Dorset. In December, I said my goodbyes to my new colleagues at Roneo and our family headed south into one of the biggest snow blizzards for decades, to a council house that we had swapped with another family, who took over our house in Shire. Jobs were not easy, especially in the countryside, but I eventually found employment as a trainee receptionist at the historic Kings Head Hotel in Wimborne, Dorset.

## HAPPY NEW YEAR!

New Year is both the end of the year, the time when the activities of the previous twelve months are summed up, and a beginning when resolutions are made for the coming year. New Year in Shirehampton, when I was growing up, was a noisy time. At midnight, if we could stay up that late, neighbors would be out in the streets banging metal dustbin lids together shouting "Happy New Year!" Then all the boats down at Avonmouth Docks would sound their horns. First one, then another and another until it sounded as if God had both hands and feet on a giant, church organ. It seemed to go on and on for ages. It was a tremendous and fantastic noise! It made the hair on your arms stand straight up! Gradually, first one horn, then another would stop until all that could be heard was some soft tooting from the tugs. Then all was quiet again and most folks would make their way to bed.

At such times I would wonder what I would be when I grew up. Little did I know about all the wonderful things I would do in my life. After Primary and Secondary school, I would work for a while as a secretary before training and working as a nurse and social worker. I would continue my education up to the Ph.D. level. There would be travel around the world: France, Canada, the USA, Colombia, Kenya, Russia, the Dominican Republic, Australia and New Zealand. I would marry three times; have no children of my own but care for hundreds of other people's children as a nurse and social worker. I would become stepmother to seven children from three marriages.

My employment would range from office worker to residential social worker to medical researcher, then to parapsychologist, journalist, administrator, and writer. My life would eventually take me from the cold dampness of England to the tropical climes of South America, to the humidity of New Jersey summers, then on to the scorching heat of the Nevada desert in the US. Perhaps my remaining travels will take me back to the British Isles or somewhere more exotic, you never know!

But as a child in Shirehampton all these adventures were ahead of me and I was content to daydream, explore, run, shout, jump, and play the days away.

The working-class society I grew up in expected me to settle down and marry or at least work in the same jobs as my parents. But I was a stubborn child and realized that there was more to life than what was expected of us Shire kids. After all, we were the new Elizabethans!

Printed in Great Britain
by Amazon